To Shule [...]
with [...]
regards and fond
memories

Ken Wensley
Oct 1, 1971

A Man's Home,
a Man's Castle

BY THE SAME AUTHOR

Black Victory: *Carl Stokes*
and the Winning of Cleveland

A Man's Home, a Man's Castle

KENNETH G. WEINBERG

Introduction by Haywood Burns

The McCall Publishing Company

New York

Copyright © 1971 by Kenneth G. Weinberg

Published simultaneously in Canada by Doubleday
Canada Ltd., Toronto.
Library of Congress Catalog Card Number: 71–144814
ISBN 0–8415–0109–2

The McCall Publishing Company
230 Park Avenue, New York, N.Y. 10017

PRINTED IN THE UNITED STATES OF AMERICA

Design by Margaret F. Plympton

To *Helen, Janet, Hugh,* and *John*

Contents

Foreword

The house of everyone is to him as his castle and fortress, as well for his defense against injury and violence as for his repose.

Sir Edward Coke
1552–1634

Sir Edward Coke was not running for public office when he uttered his famous dictum in the first quarter of the seventeenth century. He was, rather, as Lord Chief Justice of England, asserting that all Englishmen had certain basic rights at common law which deserved protection, even against the royal prerogative of King James. This revolutionary concept eventually landed Lord Coke in the Tower of London where he at least managed to keep his head, something that many highly placed inmates of the Tower were not able to do in those days. Coke's dictum became firmly imbedded in Anglo-Saxon common law, was carried intact to the colonies, and then into this country, where today the defense "a man's home is his castle" will excuse a homicide from punishment—if the accused can show that he was reasonably put in apprehension of his life by an attack upon his castle and fortress.

"Your home is your castle—protect it," said George P. Mahoney over and over again in the state of Maryland in

1966. What Mahoney, a Democratic candidate for governor, meant by this phrase in 1966 was not exactly what Coke had in mind in 1600; however, the voters of Maryland seem to understand very well the code words of our times: Mahoney's slogan told the whites of Maryland that the candidate would protect them from the blacks in their state. The whites heard and responded and George P. Mahoney, who in six previous races had been rejected by Maryland voters, became the Democratic nominee for governor. Mahoney was defeated in the general election by a former PTA president named Spiro Agnew, who said nothing on the housing issue. Alongside the reactionary Mahoney, Agnew was considered a liberal or even a radic-lib by many Maryland voters. Thus are vice-presidents made. History does, indeed, play bad jokes.

Mahoney lost, but the power of his slogan was demonstrated in Florida, where it helped Claude R. Kirk, Jr., a relatively unknown Republican, obtain enough anxious white votes to become governor of that state.

Reassuring white voters that their homes were their castles was not a practice limited to demagogic opportunists. In 1967 in Cleveland, Seth Taft, a pillar of the establishment and the grandson of a President of the United States, could not resist using the magic code words in his unsuccessful mayoralty campaign against Carl Stokes.

It is fashionable today among many whites and blacks, whether out of ideology, expediency, or despair, to claim that separation of the races is not necessarily a bad thing but may, in fact, be wise, useful, desirable, and, possibly, inevitable. This may or may not be so, but one thing is clear—white America has, for one hundred years, used every resource at its command to ensure that the races were kept separate. It is really not possible to make a judgment about the feasibility of an integrated America, because the whites of this country have been so successful in preventing integration. First there was separation by force of law, then separation by agreement among whites, open or in secret, then separation by terror and intimidation and finally separation by ruse and artifice and by shoddy political slogans such as "a man's home is his castle."

In 1925, in the state of Michigan, Ossian Sweet, a black physician, believed that *his* home was his castle and he tried to defend it, as Coke said he should, against injury and violence. The people of Michigan did not respond by electing Ossian Sweet to public office. Instead they did their best to send Sweet, his wife, two brothers, and seven friends to the penitentiary for life.

Sweet, his family, and friends had gathered in Sweet's newly purchased home—in a white neighborhood in Detroit— to protect the home from a mob that had assembled to drive the unwelcome blacks from the neighborhood. A white man had been killed by a gun shot which may or may not have been fired from inside the Sweet house and all eleven occupants of the house had been indicted for first-degree murder.

The National Association for the Advancement of Colored People, which, in 1917, had won, or thought it had won, a significant victory in the United States Supreme Court, when housing segregation laws were declared unconstitutional, now saw an opportunity to strike a blow at segregation by terror and the association persuaded Clarence Darrow to represent the defendants. Clarence Darrow was America's best, and best-known, criminal lawyer. He had contributed as much, in his way, to the development of American criminal law as Lord Coke had contributed to the development of English common law. Though Darrow was never required to serve time in the Tower for his efforts, the sovereign state of California did try to send him to prison for an alleged bribery of a juror. He was acquitted of the charge, but only after taking over the defense, himself, from the lawyer he had hired to represent him.

Darrow, in 1925, was sixty-eight years old and had spent most of the two preceding years in two of the most strenuous cases of his long career—the Scopes trial in Tennessee and the Loeb–Leopold case in Chicago—but he saw temptations in the Sweet case that he could not resist. Though Darrow was a lifelong atheist, the zeal with which he attacked folly wherever he found it was that of a missionary; and what had happened in Detroit and was happening to race relations throughout the country in that decade of the Ku Klux Klan seemed to Darrow to be very foolish indeed.

Darrow was at his best when he could represent not only a client but a cause. He had used a murder trial forum in 1905 in Idaho to argue for the right of miners to organize; he had used the Scopes "monkey trial" to argue for the freedom to teach and the freedom to learn; he had argued in the Loeb–Leopold case for the use of psychiatry in the administration of criminal law—he now welcomed the opportunity to expose racial prejudice to the scrutiny of a courtroom proceeding. "I wanted to make converts," he wrote. "I wished to make everyone reasonable and tolerant."

An impossible goal, to be sure, but neither before the Sweet trials in 1925 and 1926 nor since that time has the whole sorry spectacle of race relations in America been laid so bare in a court of law. Darrow wanted badly to teach America a lesson and he thought for a while that he had succeeded. In a speech to the NAACP in New York, shortly after the second Sweet trial in 1926, the usually pessimistic Darrow voiced a cautious, optimistic hope that the Sweet trials had marked a turning point in race relations in this country.

Long before the end of Darrow's life it was clear that this was not the case. *The People* v. *Ossian Sweet, et al.* could not be heard above the roar of the twenties. The trials passed virtually unnoticed in the decade which produced the Scopes trial, Loeb–Leopold, Hall–Mills, Sacco–Vanzetti, and the St. Valentine's Day massacre. *The New York Times,* which for years has been giving us all the news that's fit to print and then some, carried only a few short items on the entire affair.

It has been almost half a century since the Sweet trials and Darrow has been dead for over thirty years. But were he alive he would not be at all surprised by black power and white backlash; by the trouble in Detroit, Newark, Watts, Hough, and Harlem; by George P. Mahoney, Lester Maddox, and George Wallace; by Malcolm X and Eldridge Cleaver. What happened in Detroit in 1925 served as a dress rehearsal for it all, and Darrow foresaw it—in that courtroom in Detroit.

Darrow had been attracted to the case because, so far as he knew, no black man in this country charged with killing a white man had ever successfully pleaded self-defense. He also had a tremendous admiration for the intelligence and courage of Ossian Sweet and his brothers, something that Darrow was not able to say about many of his other clients. The Sweets were, indeed, a remarkable family. It took courage just short of reckless abandon for blacks to defy a white mob in Detroit in 1925. The Ku Klux Klan had reached the zenith of its power in Detroit in that very year and had nearly elected its candidate for mayor. Race riots had recently occurred in Omaha, Tulsa, East St. Louis, and Chicago, and the NAACP had charged that at least forty blacks had unjustifiably, if not wantonly, been killed by Detroit policemen in the preceding year.

Nothing in the background of the well-educated, middle-class, financially successful Ossian Sweet suggested that he would ever play the role of a trail-blazing "black militant," or that he was interested in anything more than buying a decent home for himself and his family. But when trouble came he did not run away from it. He and his brothers anticipated the Black Panthers by thirty years, when they provided for themselves the defense they were not able to get from the Detroit Police Department.

What really threatened white society's concept of law and order in 1925 was not the alleged shooting of a white by a black, but the far more dangerous act of a black man refusing to be intimidated by whites. Clarence Darrow knew that was the real crime that Ossian Sweet was being tried for, and he was determined to make white America aware of the attitudes and prejudices brought to that Detroit courtroom; to warn of the consequences if those attitudes and prejudices were not changed. Clarence Darrow, the atheist, was also Clarence Darrow, the prophet. But no one was listening in 1925. Prophets deserve to be listened to.

Author's Note

On May 18, 1926, Clarence Darrow began his closing argument for the defense in the second trial of the Sweet murder case. He spoke for almost eight hours. Excerpts from his argument appear at the beginning of each chapter.

Introduction

If We Must Die

If we must die—let it not be like hogs
Hunted and penned in an inglorious spot.
While round us bark the mad and hungry dogs,
Making their mock at our accursed lot.
If we must die—oh, let us nobly die,
So that our precious blood may not be shed
In vain; then even the monsters we defy
Shall be constrained to honor us though dead!
Oh, Kinsmen! We must meet the common foe;
Though far outnumbered, let us show us brave,
And for their thousand blows deal one deathblow!
What though before us lies the open grave?
Like men we'll face the murderous, cowardly pack,
Pressed to the wall, dying, but fighting back!

For many in white America, circa 1919, black poet Claude
McKay's assertiveness and defiance was too much to abide.
On its publication, the poem "If We Must Die" was roundly
denounced in every quarter of the nation. To show the country just what these blacks were coming to, Senator Henry
Cabot Lodge read the poem into the record of Congress;
while everywhere it was cited as evidence of a new spirit of
resistance on the part of black people.

In the years immediately following World War I, as in all years since they were stolen from green Africa, American blacks did indeed die "like hogs," butchered in this or that "inglorious spot." More than seventy blacks were lynched during the first years of the postwar period—including ten soldiers, several still in uniform. "The mad and hungry dogs" publicly burned fourteen blacks, eleven of whom were burned alive. In the infamous "Red Summer" of 1919, race riots flared in every part of the country, and by the end of the year, some twenty-five American cities had been ravaged.

Though violence against blacks was hardly new to the American scene, many were surprised and alarmed at the way in which blacks were responding to the rising onslaughts of terror. Instead of continued passivity and acceptance of their lot as an outnumbered and despised people, blacks were indeed "fighting back!" One of the bloodiest riots of the twentieth century was precipitated in East St. Louis, Illinois, in July, 1917, when blacks, grown tired of being set upon and beaten by white mobs, fired upon a Ford car believed to contain the persons who had shot up black homes earlier that evening. The two dead white men inside the car turned out to be police department plainclothes detectives. The riot started the next morning. A few weeks later in Houston, Texas, approximately one hundred black soldiers broke into an army ammunition storage room and marched on the city's police station to confront Houston's white police—who had earlier in the day abused a black woman while arresting her and then beaten a black soldier who had attempted to intercede on her behalf. The Longview, Texas, riot of 1919 started when blacks gunned down several white men who invaded the black section of town hunting a black schoolteacher who had supposedly sent a press release to the black *Chicago Defender* concerning the lynching of a black during the previous month. The Elaine, Arkansas, riot of 1919 was set off when white lawmen shot into a black church and the blacks returned the fire, killing a deputy sheriff. The Tulsa, Oklahoma, riot of 1921 was set off when a group of blacks took arms and went to the local jail to protect an accused black against a threatened lynching. And so it was in the immediate postwar years and on into the early 1920s; individually and in groups, blacks were standing up with fierce determination, and were meeting white force with black force.

Of course, white alarmists notwithstanding, neither the McKay philosophy of retaliatory violence nor its practice was new to the black community. At every step along the long road there have been blacks who have exhorted their "Kinsmen" to fight back, and blacks who have heeded the call to armed resistance or self-defense. What made this spirit particularly notable in the early 1920s was the vigor with which it was espoused and propagated by a new group of black intellectuals, and the stark contrast it presented to the overall quiescence of pre-World War I black America, cowed and trampled by the ascendant white racism. A confluence of several factors accounts for this new assertiveness. Black Americans played a significant role in the war to "make the world safe for democracy," only to return from defeating the enemy abroad to find the old enemy within very much alive. As the Chicago *Challenge* magazine observed, after describing the burning alive of a young black boy in Mississippi:

> The "German Hun" is beaten but the world is made no safer for Democracy. Humanity has been defended but lifted no higher. Democracy never will be safe in America until these occurrences are made impossible either by the execution of the law or with double barrel shot guns.... I hate every Hun, and the worst I know are the ones that thrive under the free institutions of America.

In fact, far from the situation improving after the war, the virulence of white racism became more extreme as the Ku Klux Klan and other racist groups experienced a resurgence to deal with the "uppity" black doughboy who, back from the liberal contamination of France, now seemed to the racists to threaten whites' jobs, neighborhoods, and racial integrity. In addition, blacks in this period were discovering a new pride in blackness, fired on the one hand by the intellectuals of the "Negro Renaissance" and on another by the preachings of Marcus Garvey, a black Moses who communicated to the black masses for the first time how beautiful they were. Also helping to create the mood of the times, alongside race enmity and race pride, was the deep frustration many blacks felt over their attempts to make a good life for themselves in the North. After 1910, black migration had grown apace as blacks streamed out of the rural South into the northern urban centers, each bearing his private dream. They came by the tens of thousands. In Chicago alone, the black population more than doubled between 1910 and 1920. In the years immediately following the war, experience fell far short of expectations. There were fewer jobs than there had been in wartime, and even more critical was the competition for space. Blacks were penned in enclaves in increasingly overcrowded ghetto conditions, charged exorbitant rents, and blocked by ruses—legal and extralegal—from crossing the line to live in the white man's territory.

In many ways, Dr. Ossian Sweet was a perfect representative of the so-called New Negro—young, aggressive, proud. He neither asked for nor gave any quarter. He would not look for trouble, but he would claim what was rightfully his—including the right to burst out of the ghetto and live where his money (if not his neighbors) would allow. Up from the soil of a Deep South farm, and laboring at menial tasks, he had made his way through college and medical school and had gone on to extensive travel and study in Europe. Finally, while still in his twenties, he had established himself as one of the leading black physicians in Detroit. It was difficult for whites to view Ossian Sweet as the dumb but nevertheless happy and passive black. It was easy for blacks to identify with Dr. Sweet and with those of his family and friends who were around him on that fateful day when the ugly mob surged in front of his newly purchased house, and when, "pressed to the wall," the blacks fought back.

In many ways, the trial of these eleven blacks transcended

their actions or importance as individuals and gave dramatic
focus to some of the major domestic issues gripping America
at that time. It epitomized an era, much as the Scopes trial—
another case in which Clarence Darrow was defense counsel—had a short time before, or as the Chicago conspiracy
trial was to do many years later at the close of the 1960s. In
many ways, a society, its mores, and its assumptions were on
trial. The Sweet case, largely through the testimony and
involvement of the NAACP's Walter White, laid bare the
American social situation—patterns of black migration, forma-
tion of the northern urban ghetto, prevalence of lynching,
white attitudes, and black aspirations.

The single most important issue which was crystallized in
the Sweet case was the right of black self-defense in America.
The ancient and elemental common-law right of self-defense
has long been enshrined in Anglo-American jurisprudence and
folkways. It was taken for granted in the America of the 1920s
that a man had a right to defend himself and his home against
violent attack. It is unlikely that had a black man been killed
as part of a mob menacing a white householder there would
even have been a trial. However, whereas it may have been
taken for granted that this is a man's right, it has not always
been taken for granted in America that blacks are men. There
is with this right, as with so many other rights, the unspoken
corollary that it does not apply to blacks. Blacks asserting and
acting upon a right of self-defense are too threatening for
many in the dominant society to countenance. In a caste-
ridden society built upon force, the assertion of the right of the
lower caste to use counterforce disturbs the fundamental order.
Black self-defense is then viewed as a kind of aggression, an
assault upon the established and expected modes of behavior
upon which the power arrangements depend. This continues
to be true today in a nation permeated with racist social
assumptions. What Dr. Sweet should have done as a good
slave was to submit to the wishes of the whites around him.
His failure to do so meant *he* was the cause of the trouble,
not the white "monsters" who attacked his home. Dr. Sweet

should have played his role and returned to his "place." He didn't. And as so often happens, the victim wound up on trial, while the criminals went free.

In testifying before the President's Commission on Civil Disorders in 1967, Dr. Kenneth B. Clark, the distinguished scholar, remarked:

> I read that report . . . of the 1919 riot in Chicago, and it is as if I were reading the report of the investigating committee on the Harlem riot of '35, the report of the investigating committee on the Harlem riot of '43, the report of the McCone Commission on the Watts riot.

In much the same way one cannot read the story of the Sweet case without feeling "We've been there before, we're going through that again." There is much about the case and the administration of justice that remains all too familiar. But that should not be so surprising, since the law reflects the society, and since the America of today is not so very different from the America of Dr. Sweet's time—or any other time.

In looking at the Sweet case, we see the politics of justice very much at play—police, prosecutors, and judge vibrating in sympathy with the political tremors around them. Also, in 1925 even as now, blacks of varying degrees of opinion wrestled with the question of the desirability of having a white radical lawyer, no matter how good, defending an out-spoken black who has come under white society's fire. Political trials still command a gallery of supporters who come to observe and boost the morale of defendants and defense team. Judges still systematically use bail for political purposes—just as with the Sweet defendants—keeping the unpopular accused behind bars for months and even years, knowing full well that the only legitimate purpose of bail is to assure the appearance of the defendant at trial. Black defendants are still processed through a grossly disproportionate *white* system of justice. They are still tried by middle-aged, middle-class, white jurors, while their black peers, if they are placed on the jury rolls in the first place, are systematically excluded by the prosecutors' time-honored, Supreme Court-approved use of the peremptory challenge. A quarter of a century later, good lawyers still find it necessary to use the *voir dire* (questioning of the jury panel from whom jurors are selected) to educate white Americans to society's ills and to their own racism. The similarities between Clarence Darrow's conduct of the *voir dire* in the Sweet case and Charles Garry's conduct of the *voir dire* in the Huey Newton case are striking. As in the Sweet case, we are still documenting fabrication of evidence by the police in order to turn the machinery of justice to their own ends. And we are still seeing the nature of their involvement with groups who pose a threat against which, as police, they are supposed to move. As in the Sweet case, the often nebulous catch-all charge of "conspiracy" is still being employed to charge groups of unpopular defendants when evidence of substantive crimes is in scant supply or nonexistent. In short, the Sweet case is a very American case.

The Sweet case should be an excellent object lesson to blacks about the manner in which the awesome machinery of the state is rolled up, put in place, and fired on blacks who step too far out of line, and who refuse to let white America define their "place." It is the lesson of Jack Johnson, Marcus Garvey, Muhammad Ali, and Angela Davis. It is well to remember that while Dr. Sweet eventually enjoyed some measure of success in the courts, white power—official and unofficial—saw to it that his victory was a hollow one. But the Sweet case should also be an object lesson to a white America that persists in maintaining a vertical relationship over blacks, a lesson that shows that there are blacks who are willing to make the price of such a relationship very dear. In ever-increasing numbers there are blacks who—like Ossian Sweet—will pick up the gun if the choice becomes, in his terms, "to die like a man or live a coward."

Haywood Burns
National Director
National Conference of Black Lawyers

PART I

I

Dr. Sweet Buys a House

If the Court please, Gentlemen of the Jury: You have listened so long and patiently that I do not know whether
you are able to stand much more. . . .

I shall begin about where my friend Mr. Moll began
yesterday. He says lightly, gentlemen, that this isn't a race
question, this is a murder case. We don't want any prejudice; we don't want the other side to have any. Race and
color have nothing to do with this case. This is a case of
murder. Now, let's see; I am going to try to be as fair as
I can with you gentlemen; still I don't mind being watched
at that. I just want you to give such consideration to what
I say as you think it is worth. I insist that there is nothing
but prejudice in this case; that if it was reversed and
eleven white men had shot and killed a black while protecting their home and their lives against a mob of blacks,
nobody would have dreamed of having them indicted. I
know what I am talking about, and so do you. They
would have been given medals instead. . . .

Was Mr. Moll right when he said that color has nothing
to do with the case? There is nothing in this case but the
feeling of prejudice which has been carefully nourished
by the white man until he doesn't know that he has it
himself. While I admire and like my friend Moll very
much, I can't help criticizing his argument. I suppose I
may say what old men are apt to say, in a sort of patron-

izing way, that his zeal is due to youth and inexperience.
That is about all we have to brag about as we get older,
so we ought to be permitted to do that. Let us look at
this case.

Henry Ford, who said "History is bunk," could not have
cared less that a Cadillac beat a Ford to Detroit by two hundred years. Nor could Antoine de la Mothe Cadillac, who
founded the city in 1701, have foreseen that, two centuries
later, Henry Ford would put Americans on wheels so they
could better pursue their symbol of the American Dream—
a Cadillac. On the day in 1914 that the Ford Motor Company
announced it would henceforth pay the unheard-of wage of
five dollars per day, the Detroit police and fire departments
had to help control the crowds that stormed the company
gates to share in the treasure. There was no need to hurry.
The assembly lines were rolling and where Ford went, Dodge
and General Motors were sure to follow. There were not only
enough jobs for all the central-, eastern- and southern-European
immigrants who had been washed all the way to Detroit
in the turn-of-the-century wave of immigration, but there
were jobs left over for poor black and white southern Americans who were drawn north by the chance to make in one
day what most of them could not earn down home for a
week's work.

War production in 1917 and 1918 superseded automobile
production, but at war's end the country's transportation revolution began in earnest. More and more workers were needed
to build more and more cars. Customers were easier to find
than workers. Immigration restrictions had cut off the supply
of cheap European labor and on January 1, 1919, Henry Ford
raised his minimum wage to six dollars for a ten-hour day.
Still more workers were needed; Ford and his competitors

set up employment offices throughout the South, where bad boll-weevil years in 1917 and 1918 had created widespread unemployment in the cotton industry. Black southerners would have gone to Detroit for much less than five dollars a day, even if they had been told by the employment agents, which they were not, that while Detroit offered them grand new factories to work in, there were no houses to live in and black newcomers to the city were expected to find whatever housing they could within the three east-side wards known as Paradise Valley. This seemed to matter little at first because doubling, or even tripling, with a relative or friend in Paradise Valley was still, in most cases, more comfortable than a tenant farm shack without plumbing. But the exodus intensified. One Detroit charity worker, presumably an inveterate train watcher, reported that two thousand Negro immigrants arrived in Detroit by train during a single week in May, 1920.

Soon there was trouble in Paradise. By 1925, Detroit's blacks constituted over 7 percent of the population, but they were still squeezed into 1 percent of the housing. Sixty-six percent of the black population had been crowded into Paradise Valley and by 1925 it was clear that paradise was lost—Detroiters began referring to the district as Black Bottom.

The housing situation had deteriorated even from the low point described in the 1919 report of the Research Bureau of Associated Charities of Detroit:

> There was not a single vacant house or tenement in the several Negro sections of this city. The majority of Negroes are living under such crowded conditions that three or four families in an apartment is the rule rather than the exception. Seventy-five percent of the Negro homes have so many lodgers that they are really hotels. Stables, garages and cellars have been converted into rooms for Negroes. The pool rooms and gambling clubs are beginning to charge for the privilege of sleeping on pool room tables overnight.

It is difficult to tell whether the Associated Charities was concerned about people sleeping on pool tables or being charged for it.

Housing for blacks in Detroit was still in the pool table stage when Ossian Sweet, a twenty-six-year-old physician, decided to settle in this city in 1921. Fresh from Howard University Medical School in Washington, D.C., Sweet decided that Detroit, with fewer than fifty black doctors to serve the fastest-growing black community in the country, would be a good place, as he said, to "make a little money and get ahead in the world."

Dr. Sweet was no stranger to Detroit, having spent several summers—while he was a student at Wilberforce Academy and Wilberforce University in Ohio—as a bellhop on lake steamers traveling between Cleveland and Detroit. He had gone to Wilberforce at fourteen from Orlando, Florida, where he had been born in 1895. His tenant farmer parents had five other children, none so exotically named as Ossian. Though it is doubtful that his parents were students of Celtic literature, Ossian Sweet liked to claim that he was the only man in America named after a fourth-century Irish warrior-lord.

He had worked his way through Wilberforce by waiting on tables, shoveling snow, and firing furnaces, and at Howard Medical School he had supported himself by hiring out to parties as a waiter and bartender. Upon graduation, he interned at the Freedman's Hospital in Washington before setting up his practice in Detroit. It was not necessary for the associated charities to welcome Ossian Sweet to Detroit. Not only had he worked his way through high school, college, and medical school, but he had managed to save money while doing it. His practice immediately thrived and in 1922, when he married Gladys Mitchell, he decided to combine his honeymoon with a year of travel and study.

After taking graduate courses in pediatrics and gynecology at the University of Vienna in 1923, Sweet took his wife on a tour of Italy and North Africa, and then went to Paris to study radiology at the Curie Institute. Gladys Sweet was pregnant when the Sweets arrived in Paris and Dr. Sweet allocated 300 francs from his rapidly dwindling capital to a fund-raising drive by the American Hospital in Paris, an institution then supported largely by American funds for the use of Americans in Paris. Sweet expected that his child would be born there and the 300 francs might earn a little special attention.

Throughout Europe and North Africa, and in Paris, the Sweets had been recognized for what they were: better educated, more cultivated, and more intelligent than the average American abroad. Gladys Sweet had attended Detroit Junior College and Detroit Teachers' College after being graduated from the Detroit public school system, and she and her husband, both of them young, handsome, and articulate, were indeed impressive representatives of their country. But when it was time for the birth of the Sweets' baby in June, 1924, the American Hospital in Paris, whose white beds had never accommodated black bodies, reacted as a white American hospital would anywhere in 1924, and refused admittance to Gladys Sweet. The baby, a girl, was born in a French hospital, and Sweet always considered it a special irony that the only instance of discrimination encountered in a year and a half abroad occurred in an American hospital.

In the fall of 1924, Sweet returned to Detroit to resume his medical practice. With his wife and baby daughter he moved into the small house owned and occupied by Gladys Sweet's mother. Mrs. Mitchell had escaped Paradise Valley several years earlier by moving to a partially integrated neighborhood on the near northeast side of town. But the house was much too small for two families and in the spring of 1925 the Sweets went house-hunting. Even if there were houses available in Paradise Valley, the Sweets would not have considered moving back there. It had become a crime-infested slum where absentee landlords packed more and more families into inadequate and unrepaired dwellings and where the city permitted speakeasies and houses of prostitution to flourish.

Ossian Sweet was not trying to prove anything. As his brother Otis later said, "He wasn't looking for trouble. He just wanted to bring up his little girl in good surroundings." Good surroundings were not to be found in Paradise Valley in 1925, and Sweet had little reason to expect that trouble of any kind would result from a simple real estate transaction. Blacks had, in the previous two years, purchased homes in various white sections of the city without incident and Mrs. Sweet's parents had lived peacefully for several years with their white neighbors.

Such optimism might have seemed misplaced in 1925, the year in which the Ku Klux Klan, with an estimated 100,000 members, reached the peak of its power in Detroit. But blacks, in 1925, were rather far down the KKK's hate list, ranking no better than fourth behind Catholics, foreigners, and Jews. Most of the Klan's efforts that year seemed to be concentrated on defeating John W. Smith, a Roman Catholic, who was running to succeed himself as mayor and against whom the Klan was strongly supporting Charles W. Bowles, with whose color, nationality, and religion the Klan could find no fault.

Accordingly, Sweet almost felt himself to be among friends when he began negotiating for the purchase of a house on the northeast side, in an area populated mostly by foreign-born factory workers. The Michigan Klan had grown from xenophobic origins in a Detroit organization known as SYMWA—Spend Your Money With Americans—and still had an obsessive fear of foreigners. In spite of the Michigan law prohibiting masked parades, the Klan had marched through the neighborhood in splendid hooded anonymity only a month before Sweet bought his house. The KKK wanted to demonstrate its Americanism to all those foreigners. Sweet was, at least, certain that his neighbors would not confuse him with a Klansman.

When Sweet's friend, Lucius Riley, a black real estate agent, had first shown him the house at 2905 Garland Avenue on the corner of Charlevoix Street, Sweet had made it a point to examine conspicuously the outside of the house in broad daylight and to sit on the front porch with Mrs. Edward Smith, the white owner of the house. Sweet assumed it would be quite clear to any curious neighbor that the black man showing so much interest in 2905 Garland Avenue was neither a handy-man, a garbage man, nor a deliveryman.

Sweet and Riley were also encouraged by the fact that Mrs. Smith was married to a black man who had lived in the house with her for two years without shocking the sensibility of the neighborhood. But this, apparently, was only because the neighbors had not realized that Mr. Smith was black. He was very light skinned and, since the residents of Garland and Charlevoix could not conceive of a marriage between a white woman and a black man, Edward Smith was taken for white. He himself seemed to have some doubt as to his color. When he was later asked by the prosecutor whether he was a Negro he answered, "I am supposed to be."

During the month of May, Sweet visited the house several times and was not aware of any unrest in the neighborhood. So, for $18,500 ($3,000 down, the balance by mortgage) Ossian Sweet became the owner of his first home. Comparable homes in the area had been bought by whites in the previous year for less than $15,000, certainly a more accurate reflection of the market value on the street. The Detroit newspapers later referred to the area as "the exclusive Garland Avenue district," but Garland Avenue was not Grosse Pointe, though it shared the same determination to exclude black neighbors.

Sweet did not object to the premium price but he was later to say, "If I had known how bitter that neighborhood was going to be, I wouldn't have taken that house as a gift."

Under the terms of the purchase agreement, the Smiths were to continue to occupy the house until July. Long before then it was clear that Dr. Sweet had made a poor diagnosis of the temper of the neighborhood, which almost immediately began to run a high temperature from racial fever. A Waterworks Improvement Association was formed as soon as it was learned that Mrs. Smith had really done it—in spite of the threats. The Waterworks Park neighborhood had never before seen the need for an improvement association and, as the club's members were later freely to admit, the improvement in mind was to keep Dr. Sweet from occupying his house.

II

The Mecca
of the Colored Race

Dancy says there were six or seven thousand colored people here sixteen years ago. And seventy-one thousand five years ago. Gentlemen, why are they here? They came here as you came here, under the laws of trade and business, under the instincts to live; both the white and the colored, just the same; the instincts of all animals to propagate their kind, the feelings back of life and on which life depends. They came here to live. Your factories were open for them. Mr. Ford hired them. The automobile companies hired them. Everybody hired them. They were willing to give them work, weren't they? Every one of them. You and I are willing to give them work, too. We are willing to have them in our houses to take care of the children and do the rough work that we shun ourselves. We invited them; pretty nearly all of the colored population has come to Detroit in the last fifteen years; most of them, anyhow. They have always had a corner on the meanest jobs. The city must grow, or you couldn't brag about it. The colored people must live somewhere. Everybody is willing to have them live somewhere else. The people at the corner of Garland and Charlevoix would be willing to have them go to some other section. They would be willing to have them buy a place next to

Mrs. Dodge's house; but most of them haven't got money enough to do that; none that I know of. Everybody would be willing to have them go somewhere else. Somewhere they must live. Are you going to kill them? Are you going to say that they can work but they can't get a place to sleep? They can toil in the mill, but can't eat their dinner at home. We want them to build automobiles for us, don't we? We even let them become our chauffeurs. Oh, gentlemen, what is the use! You know it is wrong. Everyone of you know it is wrong. You know that no man in conscience could blame a Negro for almost anything. Can you think of these people without shouldering your own responsibilities?

During the eighteenth century there were never more than a few hundred blacks in Detroit, all of them slaves. With the growth of the abolitionist movement in the nineteenth century, Detroit's black population grew rapidly with an influx of escaped slaves, who stopped and stayed on their way to Canada or crossed the river for a brief sojourn in another country until it was safe to return to Detroit. By 1850, there were over 2,000 Negroes in the city, none of whom were slaves. By 1910, there were 6,000 blacks out of a total population of 470,000. The automobile boom and the First World War swelled the black community to 41,000 out of 1,000,000; a substantial minority but posing no real threat to Detroit's various ethnic groups, such as the 100,000-member Polish community.

But the migration continued. The siren song tooted by Henry Ford's Model T lured more and more southern blacks. By 1925, the black population had doubled to 80,000 out of a total of 1,200,000. Out of 20,000 employed black males, 10,000 worked for Henry Ford, and for those who did not work for

Ford or one of the other auto companies it was back to the old elevator, shoeshine stand, or porter's broom. There were few other opportunities open to blacks. In addition to Ossian Sweet's fifty medical colleagues, there were only twenty black dentists, forty black teachers out of a total of 6,000, and, most significantly, only fourteen black policemen out of a force of 3,000.

Whatever their occupation, there was no housing for blacks. There was virtually no new construction in the overcrowded ghetto and there were actually fewer housing units available for Negroes in 1925 than there had been in 1920, since many ghetto houses had been replaced by gas stations, whorehouses, speakeasies, and gambling joints. Even the lodgers were taking in lodgers and there was no space left on the pool table tops. In 1925 the seams finally burst and blacks began escaping from the ghetto in large numbers, as their ancestors had escaped across the Detroit River a hundred years earlier.

It was a bad year for integrated housing. The mayoralty race began to focus on race and religion. During the summer the Klan had burned a cross in Mayor Smith's front yard and a prominent Protestant minister had called for tar and feathers for anyone voting for Smith. Smith's religion and his opposition to the Volstead Act alone would have been more than enough to incur the enmity of the KKK. But what really could not be tolerated was his strange notion that Detroit's black population had some rights. This seemed to startle and frighten at least some Detroiters. The Greater Detroit Realtors Committee widely distributed reprints of an article which had appeared in the *Birmingham Gazette*:

200,000 NEGROES PLAN PILGRIMAGE TO DETROIT—CALAMITY
THREATENS PLANTERS THROUGHOUT THE COTTON BELT

A wave of restlessness similar to that which overcame the Negro during the stirring days of 1914–1918 is becoming more apparent each day, as information streams into this office from its numerous correspondents throughout the great cotton belt.

Cotton growers are alarmed and incensed at this condition and much speculation is rife as to where labor will be secured to remedy this serious situation.

Northern Negro agitators have been busy during the last few weeks spreading dissension and turmoil among the colored people of this section.

Detroit, Michigan, is being held out as the "Mecca of the colored race." Protection, social equality and steady employment is promised under their present leader, Mayor John W. Smith, according to these agitators.

They sum up the situation in that great auto city by alleging that Negroes are allowed to move into white neighborhoods where they will be fully protected by the white policemen, who are at present employed by the city administration.

The Greater Detroit Realtors Committee, in explaining the distribution of this article, told Detroiters:

Many voters may be curious to know just why this committee is interested in the above article carried by the leading newspaper of the South. It is our candid opinion based on years of practical real estate experience, that if our city is deluged by this black flood of colored immigration it will decrease the value of Detroit real estate to the extent of $2,000,000,000.

It is also our opinion that such an influx of unskilled labor will produce a condition under which it will be impossible for the working man to exist.

Voters should carefully consider the above propositions.

The Detroit Real Estate Board disavowed any connection with this reprint or any knowledge of the Greater Detroit Realtors Committee. The Board, however, not only did not disavow, but passionately embraced Article 34 of the Code of Ethics of the National Association of Real Estate Boards:

A Realtor should never be instrumental in introducing

into a neighborhood a character of property or occupancy by members of any race or nationality or any individuals whose presence will be detrimental to property values in that neighborhood.

And, of course, the Board, like real estate boards throughout the country, recommended restrictive covenants and exclusive agreements as a means of "maintaining property values."

Meanwhile, back in the "mecca of the colored race," white mobs forced several black families to vacate homes in white neighborhoods in the summer of 1925. On June 22, Dr. A. L. Turner, a black physician and an acquaintance of Ossian Sweet, received a friendly neighborhood call from his new neighbors on Spokane Street, in the mostly white neighborhood to which Dr. Turner had recently moved from Warren Avenue, an all-black part of town. Dr. Turner had not been expecting company and the three thousand angry whites who gathered outside his house were clearly not the Welcome Wagon.

Dr. Turner started to breathe a little easier when the police responded rapidly to his call, but instead of dispersing the crowd, the police drove Turner and his wife back to their old house on Warren Avenue, told them to stay there if they valued their lives, and arranged for the Tireman Avenue Improvement Association, which had mobilized the mob, to redeliver all of Dr. Turner's furniture back to Warren Avenue.

Later that summer Vollington Bristol, a black undertaker, was forced from his home on American Avenue after three successive nights of demonstrations, and other blacks were run out of homes on Bangor Street and Merrill Street. The Fourth of July was celebrated with a cross-burning on Vincent Park, in front of the home of a black attorney, with a sign proclaiming "No niggers allowed in this vicinity."

Dr. Sweet was not the first black in Detroit's long, hot summer of 1925 to attempt to stand up to a white mob. On Stoepel Avenue, a fifteen-year-old white boy, Leonard Paul, was wounded by gunfire from the home of a Negro waiter, John Fletcher, while a crowd of whites was chucking at the house, lump by lump, a ton of coal that had been deposited on the sidewalk for delivery to the house next door. (Fletcher's neighbor must have been expecting an early winter to have ordered his coal in July.) Fletcher was arrested but the charges against him were dismissed before trial. There is no record of the arrest of any white in connection with this or any of Detroit's other racial incidents of that summer.

Life had been good to Ossian Sweet. His practice was thriving and he was making more money than most physicians—black or white—in Detroit. He knew no other Detroit doctor who could claim graduate studies at two universities abroad. He had a lovely wife and a healthy baby girl. When there were no immediate repercussions following the purchase of Mrs. Smith's house in June, he thought his luck was holding.

But in July, Mrs. Smith had some bad news for him. The good people of the Waterworks Park District would not tolerate a prosperous black physician with postgraduate honors, a cultivated wife, and an infant daughter, any more than they would welcome a poor, black, illiterate, cotton-belt sharecropper with ten children. Mrs. Smith, who had decided to move to California, perhaps to get as far away as possible from her neighbors, told Sweet that she had begun to receive threatening telephone calls, one warning her that they "would get her if they had to follow her to California," and another saying they "would kill the nigger" if he dared to move into the house.

Ossian Sweet was determined not to let the Detroit improvers have another victory and he refused to be intimidated. When he learned that people were threatening his life before he even moved into the house, he told his brother that he "had to die like a man or live a coward."

III

Law and Order

I don't need to go far. I don't need to travel to Florida.
I don't even need to talk about the Chicago riots—I don't
need to go to Washington or to St. Louis. Let us take
Detroit. I don't need to go far either in space or time.
Let us take this city. I know what has been done in
Chicago. I know what prejudice growing out of race
and religion has done the world over, and all through
time. I am not blaming Detroit. I am stating what has
happened, that is all. . . . It is a new idea in Detroit that
a colored man's home can be torn down about his head,
because he is black. There are some eighty thousand
blacks here now, and they are bound to reach out. . . .

They sent four policemen in the morning to help this
little family move in. They had a bedstead, a stove and
some bedding, ten guns and some ammunition, and they
had food to last them through a siege. I feel that they
should have taken less furniture and more food and guns.

The Waterworks Improvement Association was forty years
ahead of George P. Mahoney, George C. Wallace, and Spiro T.
Agnew in its use of code words to exploit racial fear. Its
high sounding by-laws, adopted at the organization meeting

in early July, used catch phrases of remarkable durability. The association's expressed purposes were:

(1) To render constructive social and civic services;

(2) To maintain a clean and healthy condition in streets and alleys;

(3) To observe the spirit of the traffic ordinances for safety and protection of residents;

(4) To cooperate with all city departments and all beneficial plans;

(5) To cooperate with the police in the maintenance of law and order; and

(6) To cooperate in the enforcement of existing property restrictions and to originate such other restrictions as would preserve and protect the locality as a respectable community.

One week after the adoption of these by-laws John Fletcher shot Leonard Paul on Stoepel Avenue and improvement associations began holding meetings all over the city. In the newspapers the shooting was portrayed as an unprovoked attack by a black upon an innocent white youth and cross-burnings became a nightly ritual.

Mayor Smith, who began to see his reelection hopes, if not his city, go up in flames, tried to calm the tension by publishing a statement in the *Detroit Free Press* on July 12:

Recent incidents of violence and attempted violence in connection with racial disagreements constitute a warning to the people of Detroit which they cannot afford to ignore. They are to be deplored, and it is a duty which rests as much upon the citizenry as upon the public officials to see that they do not grow into a condition which will be a lasting stain upon the reputation of Detroit as a law-abiding community.

The police department can have but one duty in connection with all such incidents, that is, to use its utmost endeavors, to prevent the destruction of life and property. In the performance of this duty, I trust that every police officer will be unremitting in his efforts. The law recognizes no distinction in color or race. On all occasions when the emotions are deeply stirred by controversy, the persons affected on all sides by the dispute are likely to feel that the police or other controlling forces are siding against them. I hope and believe that the police during the recent attempts to preserve law and order have done so impartially.

With the police department doing its utmost to preserve order, there is always the possibility that uncontrolled elements may reach such proportions that even these efforts will not be completely effectual. It is that fact that calls for earnest cooperation by all good citizens at this time. Curiosity seekers who go to the scenes of threatened disorder add immeasurably to the problem of preserving order. Thus, the persons innocent of ill intentions are likely to be chiefly responsible for inexcusable incidents.

The condition which faces Detroit is one which faced Washington, East St. Louis, Chicago and other large cities. The result in those cities was one which Detroit must avoid, if possible. A single fatal riot would injure this city beyond remedy.

The avoidance of further disorder belongs to the good sense of the leaders of thought in both white and colored races. The persons either white or colored who attempt to urge their fellows on to disorder and crime are guilty of the most serious offense upon the statute books. It is clear that a thoughtless individual of both races constitutes the nucleus in each disorder and it is equally clear that the inspiration for their acts comes from malign influences which are willing to go even to the limits of bloodshed to gain their ends. The police are expected to inquire and prosecute any persons active in organizing such disorder or inciting a riot. The rest of the duty for preserving order lies with the individual citizens by refraining from adding to the crowds in districts where danger exists, by refraining from discussions which may

have a tendency to incite disorder, and finally to rebuke
at once the individual agitators who are willing to risk
human life, destroy property, and ruin their city's
reputation.

This was a remarkably evenhanded statement for a terribly
lopsided situation. Reading it one would think that whites and
blacks had been equally guilty of driving each other out of
neighborhoods. The emphasis on "order" and "disorder" and
the absence of any realistic assessment of what had been happening in Detroit compels the conclusion that underlying
Mayor Smith's statement was the forlorn hope that if blacks
would only stay where they belong, order would prevail.

The issue of the *Free Press* which carried this statement also
contained the following notice, with a message much less
ambiguous than the Mayor's:

> To maintain the high standard of the residential district
> between Jefferson and Mack Avenues, a meeting has
> been called by the Waterworks Improvement Associa-
> tion for Thursday night in the Howe School Auditorium.
> Men and women of the district, which includes Cadillac,
> Hurburt, Bewick, Garland, St. Clair, and Harding Ave-
> nues, are asked to attend in self-defense.

The meeting was duly held on the fourteenth. The Howe
School Auditorium was not large enough for the seven hundred
whites who appeared and the crowd spilled over into the
schoolyard. Among those seven hundred were two detectives
from the Detroit police department, whose function was apparently to protect the mob from any black who might have been
bold enough to appear. The officers showed absolutely no con-
cern over the open incitement to violence and riot which
occurred at the meeting. The principal speaker was a representative from the Tireman Association, who described how his
group had succeeded in removing Dr. Turner from his home
and offered every assistance of his organization in doing the
same for Dr. Sweet, should he be foolish enough to try to
occupy his property. The biggest cheer of the evening came

when he told the crowd, "Where the nigger shows his head, the white must shoot."

This was the last official meeting of the Waterworks Improvement Association. There was no need for further meetings. Either law and order, waterworks style, would prevail and Ossian Sweet would stay away from the neighborhood, or he would defy the improvers and move into his house. In that event they knew what had to be done. Ossian Sweet also knew what had to be done.

Early in September, Sweet bought the first gun he had ever owned. In fact, he bought nine of them, a thirty-eight caliber Winchester rifle, a thirty-eight Marlin rifle, a double-barreled shotgun, and six thirty-two caliber revolvers. He also purchased quantities of ammunition for each weapon. Sweet had postponed moving into his new house until September, hoping that reason would return to Charlevoix and Garland. He had notified the Detroit police department that he intended to move into the house on September 8 and asked for police protection if needed. He was not encouraged by the response. The police suggested that perhaps trouble could be avoided if Sweet were to live in another neighborhood where the neighbors had no objection to his presence. In the face of Sweet's persistence the police finally gave grudging assurance that his rights would be protected. But Sweet was not reassured. It was widely suspected that the Detroit police department was extensively infiltrated with Ku Klux Klan members. The fact that seventy-five white Southerners had been added to the department in the past year did nothing to lessen that suspicion. The NAACP claimed that over three thousand Negroes had been lynched in this country in this century and had charged the Detroit police with having killed forty blacks in the preceding year. The recent history of black-white confrontation, both in Detroit and in the country, was certainly enough to dampen Sweet's usual optimism.

Though his life, to this point, had been a model of middle-class American conformity, he was not unaware of, nor unaffected by, the new spirit of militancy which black Americans had been showing since the end of the First World War. W. E. B. Du Bois had sounded the battle cry in *Crisis*, the NAACP publication, when he had warned Negroes to be prepared for armed struggle and had said, "War is hell, but there are worse things than hell, as every Negro knows."

Struggles had indeed occurred, but then, as now, most of the casualties were black. In East St. Louis in 1917, after a series of attacks by white gangs on blacks, open warfare broke out when blacks retaliated and killed two white detectives. The final body count: nine whites and thirty-nine blacks killed. In Chicago in 1919, a black teen-ager who attempted to swim ashore to a Lake Michigan beach reserved for whites was chased back into the lake and drowned. Blacks who complained to the police and demanded the arrest of two white youths allegedly involved in the drowning were themselves arrested. The resulting escalation led to fifteen white and twenty-three black deaths.

Though Ossian Sweet was almost completely free of cynicism, he was not so naïve as to believe that a medical degree could insulate him from the white man's wrath. As a medical student at Howard University, he had observed attacks on fellow black medical students by white mobs during the Washington riots of 1919 and had been deeply affected by the lynching of Dr. A. C. Jackson, a nationally known black physician, in Tulsa in 1921. The experience of Dr. Turner with the Tireman Improvement Association was only the latest reminder, if any were needed, that A. Phillip Randolph had not been overstating the case when he wrote in the *Messenger*, in 1919:

Anglo-Saxon jurisprudence recognizes the right of self-defense. . . . The black man has no rights which will be respected unless the black man forces that respect. We are consequently urging Negroes and other oppressed groups concerned with lynching and mob violence to act upon the recognized and accepted law of self-defense.

This sounded like good advice to Sweet and he decided to act on it. He set out to form his own "improvement association" and he asked his younger brothers, Otis and Henry, if some of their friends would be willing to move into the house with them and stay until the neighborhood was pacified.

Twenty-six-year-old Otis had followed Ossian to Detroit and had begun a dental practice there in 1923. As Ossian had helped Otis with the expense of dental school, so was he now helping Henry, age twenty-one, through a prelaw course at Wilberforce. Henry, who was spending the summer in Detroit, immediately recruited John Latting, a twenty-three-year-old Wilberforce student, and another twenty-three-year-old, Joe Mack, who was working as a chauffeur. Joe Mack, in turn, solicited a chauffeur friend of his, Morris Murray. It seemed likely that the most important support would come from William Davis, who had been Ossian's close friend ever since they had been at Wilberforce together. Davis, at thirty-one, had been a federal narcotics agent for six years, a job he had taken upon his discharge from the army as a captain. His military service had included combat action overseas and as a federal agent he was the only one of the group to own a gun.

D-day was set for September 8 and the plan was for Ossian and his wife to move into the house early on that day, with the others to join them at the house before dark. Neighborhood improvement in Detroit that summer had been a nighttime thing and no trouble was expected during daylight. The move, in fact, was quite peaceful. Four policemen were on hand to watch as a moving van unloaded a moderate amount of furniture and what should have seemed like an excessive amount of food for a family of three. Hidden among the furniture and unseen by the police were the guns and ammunition.

The Sweets had decided to have their infant daughter remain at Mrs. Sweet's mother's home for the time being, and after arranging their furniture in the house they settled down to await Sweet's brothers and friends and whatever else darkness might bring.

IV

Officer Schuknecht
Keeps the Peace

What did the policeman say? There were about eight policemen standing around there to protect a colored family. Two of them were from Tennessee. That ought to have helped some. I don't know where the rest came from. Some of them seemed to come from some institution, judging by the way they talked. . . . Here is another policeman, parading all the evening on this short beat. . . . "Was there anybody on the schoolhouse yard?" "There might have been four." Four, gentlemen. I wouldn't say this man lied. It takes some mentality to lie. An idiot can't lie—now I won't say the same about Schuknecht. He has some mentality; some; just some. He said, "There were probably one hundred and fifty around there." . . . Let us see how closely they were guarding the house. They did nothing. They heard no stones thrown against that house; not one of them; and yet they were not twenty feet away. . . . Not one of them heard a stone, and yet they were there to protect that home. None of them heard the broken glass, but they were there to protect that home. . . . Gentlemen, you could have looted that house and moved it away and the police would never have known it. That is the way these people were protected.

Darkness on September 8 brought more policemen. Though
the police, to a man, consistently maintained that the evenings
of September 8 and 9 in the vicinity of Garland and Charlevoix
were normal, peaceful summer evenings, the number of people
congregating near that fateful corner required a doubling of
the guard, and by early evening there were eight policemen
on duty. Exactly what they were supposed to be doing was not
clear. Officer Schellenberger's testimony was typical.

Q: Officer Schellenberger, were you out there in this
vicinity on the evening of the eighth?

A: I was.

Q: When did you go there?

A: Oh, I should say around seven-fifteen or seven-thirty.

Q: What was the occasion of your going there on the
eighth, Lieutenant?

A: Well, we had reasons to go there for the purpose
that we knew that a colored family had moved in
there, and we didn't want a reoccurrence of what
had occurred a short time ago on the West Side, and
we were taking full precaution for the purpose of if
anything should arise, we were there for the purpose
of preserving the peace, protecting life and property.

Q: How many officers were there actually with you at
that time, seven-thirty?

A: Oh, I don't know, I should say possibly seven or
eight, around there in that vicinity.

Q: There was no trouble there, was there?

A: No sir, none whatsoever.

Q: Now, you say that you knew a colored family had
moved in that house?

A: I did.

Q: You knew he moved on that morning, didn't you?

A: I did.

Q: That was the morning of the eighth?

A: It was.

Q: How many people were around that house on the night of the eighth at the time you got there? Seven-thirty?

A: I should say possibly one hundred or one hundred and fifty people.

Q: What were they doing?

A: Just standing around on the corners, that is all. Weren't doing anything.

Q: Did you hear them say anything? Did you hear anybody make any remarks about the colored family having moved in there?

A: No sir.

Q: Said nothing about it at all?

A: No sir.

Q: Just standing there and talking?

A: That is all.

.　.　.

Q: Was there any violence on the evening of the eighth?

A: No sir.

Q: Why did you anticipate trouble there?

A: Why, I wouldn't say I anticipated any trouble, it was only a precaution.

Q: Precaution because of what?

A: Because Dr. Sweet was a colored man had moved into that vicinity.

Q: You have done that whenever a colored man moves into a vicinity?

A: It is not done customarily, no.

Q: Have you ever given police protection to any house where a colored man moved in before?

A: We have never.

Q: Why did you do it in this case?

A: For the reason of what occurred in the West Side of the city a short time previous.

Q: What occurred over there?

A: White people and colored people had a little trouble there on account of a colored family moving in, property was destroyed, and a man was shot.

From Lieutenant Schellenberger's point of view, any trouble that occurred at Garland and Charlevoix, or anywhere else in Detroit in similar circumstances, would be caused not by restrictive housing practices, or intimidating white mobs, or bigotry and prejudice, but only by a "colored family moving in." Ossian Sweet's colored family had moved in, and by night-fall on September 8 his brothers and friends had joined them and had taken up positions at the windows in the unlighted house, armed with the guns Sweet had furnished them. The Sweets were, in fact, prepared for war or peace. Two young girl friends of Mrs. Sweet, who were in the decorating business, had joined the family early in the evening to help Mrs. Sweet plan the furnishing of the house. Afraid to run the gauntlet of the unfriendly crowd, they decided to spend the night at the house.

The guns were not used that night. Though much of the crowd remained throughout the night and twenty or thirty were still in the street at daybreak, it was a relatively peaceful mob, which satisfied itself by shouting threats and curses from time to time and by throwing just one barrage of rocks against the house at about 3:00 A.M.

Though no one had slept at the Sweet house on the night of the eighth, all except Ossian, his wife, and his brother Henry left the house in the morning for their daily routines. As Joe Mack and John Latting left the house, one member of the mob still in the street said to them, "The crowd had a meeting last night in the confectionery store. You fellows better watch yourselves. They say they are going to get you out of here tonight."

This threat was reported to Ossian, who decided to bring reinforcements for the night, and he asked three young friends in the insurance business, Charles Washington, Leonard Morris, and Hewitt Watson, to join the defense. They immediately agreed. It appeared to have been a wise precaution. All day long, passersby shouted "nigger" in the general direction of the house and by midafternoon the crowd began to grow again, uglier and more belligerent than it had been the day before. There is no record that the police, at any time, did any-

thing to disperse the crowd or restrain any member of it. Had
that been done on the eighth, none of the events of the ninth
would have occurred. But a colored family had moved in and
the police were determined to protect the mob from that threat
to law and order. Again, stones were thrown against the house
and the curses and threats became more frequent. Once more
the Sweet household stationed themselves at windows with
their guns. At about 8:15 P.M., Otis Sweet and William Davis,
who had not yet returned to the house, arrived in a taxi. As
they stepped out of the car, someone in the crowd shouted,
"Here's niggers. Get them! Get them!"

Sweet and Davis made it into the house under a hail of
rocks, the mob moving closer. The barrage of rocks continued.
One shattered an upstairs window, and Ossian Sweet was cut
by flying glass. Close upon the sound of shattered glass came
the sound of gunfire. The number of shots fired remained in dispute throughout the trials. It was at least six and perhaps as
many as twenty. All appear to have been fired from within the
house except for two that one of the police officers claimed to
have fired over the crowd's head.

Testimony at the trials, from both the defendants and from
members of the crowd, established beyond reasonable doubt
the rock throwing, the shouting, the threats, and the window
breaking; but Inspector Norton Schuknecht, in charge of the
police detail, was blind to everything except the shooting.
Inspector Schuknecht, and every member of his detail, began
lying one week later at the preliminary hearing, and the lying
continued throughout the two subsequent trials.

Q: At anytime on the ninth did you see any disturb-
ance?
A: I didn't.
Q: Was there any violence of any kind reported to you
which you saw?
A: There was no violence until after the shooting.
Q: You spoke of shooting, did you see or hear any
shooting?

A: I did.

Q: That was at what time?

A: About eight twenty-five in the evening.

                    •   •   •

Q: So that you, Lieutenant Schellenberger and Otto Lemhagen were down here?

A: Yes sir.

Q: You were on duty at that time?

A: Yes sir.

Q: What attracted your attention to the shooting?

A: The sudden shooting out of the house.

Q: And how many shots were fired would you say?

A: Well, I judged probably anywhere from fifteen to twenty shots fired out of the front and side windows.

Q: Now, what did you do upon hearing the shooting, seeing the shooting?

A: I told Lieutenant Schellenberger to go down and call for help. The firing had stopped. In probably fifteen to thirty seconds, the firing had stopped. I goes over to the house, comes upon the steps there, rings the bell, someone comes to the door and asked who was there. They didn't open the door. I said, "The police officer." They opened the door.

Q: Who did you see in the house?

A: I seen Dr. Sweet.

Q: Did you have any conversation with him?

A: I did.

Q: What, please?

A: All right sir, I went in there, I said, "For Christ sake, what in hell are you fellows shooting about?" "Why," he says, "they are ruining my property." I said, "What has been done?" I said, "I haven't seen a man throw a stone or I haven't heard any commotion or anything else, I haven't heard of anyone throwing a stone." "Well," he said, "I don't see Inspector McPherson around here tonight." I said, "Doctor, I was in charge last night and I am also in charge tonight." I says, "We have got men round your house, we got them in the alley, we got them on the side, and we got them on the front." Then he said, "There will be no more shooting," so I went out of the house, I don't know just how long I was in there, I may have been in there a couple of minutes. I went out of the house then, then I was informed that two men had been shot.

Q: Did you stay on the scene?

A: Yes sir. I stayed right there and it was only a few minutes afterwards that Sergeant Fairburn got up there and also Sergeant Mahlmeister got up there and I told them, I says, "They shot a couple men and we got to go and get them all," so we went in and got them all out.

.   .   .

Q: I will ask you to state whether or not you saw anything thrown at 2905 Garland at Dr. Sweet's house?

A: Not before the shooting.

Q: Did you see anyone enter on the premises or up on the lawn, or on the sidewalk in front of the house?

A: I didn't.

On cross-examination Schuknecht doggedly insisted that prior to the shooting all had been serene at Garland and Charlevoix, though he had to concede that there was somewhat more activity than usual:

Q: How many men did you have there on the ninth?

A: Same amount of men that we had there on the eighth.

Q: Eight men?

A: Eight men up until about—it was about seven-thirty when I sent in for two more men to divert traffic on Garland Avenue—one on Goethe and Garland, one on Waterloo and Garland.

Q: Had you had to station two men on that corner before to direct traffic?

A: No sir.

Q: Inspector, did you see anybody go past the corner of Charlevoix and Garland, or in the neighborhood of 2905 Garland?

A: Yes sir, quite a number of rigs parked in there.

Q: Now Inspector, you were not paying any attention to what was going on there at the house, were you?

A: Certainly, looking right at it.

Q: What was the occasion of your looking at that house at that time?

A: Nothing then.

Q: Weren't you looking at that house because that crowd was throwing stones at that house?

A: No sir, I wasn't.

Q: Weren't you looking at that house because the crowd of people on this side of the street had begun to come over here?

A: No sir, I was not.

Q: Now you said you sent these men up there for the reason that you understood that Dr. Sweet was moving in there. Is it customary to send policemen to any house where people move in the neighborhood?

A: No sir.

Q: Why did you do it in this case?

A: Why because this is a different occasion.

Q: What was there that made this occasion different from the others?

A: Because we had the experience on the West Side.

Q: In what way?

A: That is what we were trying to avoid, any trouble that took place on the West Side.

Q: Had you heard anything that made you think there would be trouble out there?

A: No sir, I didn't.

Q: Did you know Dr. Sweet?

A: No sir.

Q: Did he tell you anything peculiar about Dr. Sweet that would make you think there was trouble?

A: No sir.

Q: Why did you anticipate trouble?

A: We didn't anticipate any. We were there to stop anything if it would arise.

Q: Was there any excitement in the neighborhood?

A: No sir, there wasn't.

Q: Well then, why did you send policemen?

A: If we hadn't sent anyone there and something had happened we would have got roasted, wouldn't we?

Q: Did you see a car drive up to that residence that evening?

A: I didn't see it, but I was told there was a car come up there and two colored gentlemen got out and went in the house.

Q: Did they tell you people stood around, stoning their car, stoned the occupants of the car?

A: They didn't.

Q: What did they tell you about it?

A: Just told me a car stopped up there, I think they said it was a taxi and two men got out of it and went into Dr. Sweet's house and the car immediately drove away.

Inspector Schuknecht and his men not only tolerated but in a sense took part in the two-day siege of the Sweet house. The police did nothing to discourage the mob and violence became inevitable. It was not at all inevitable, however, that whites would be the victims of that violence. It was supposed to be the other way around.

Accordingly, Detroit was outraged. The newspapers portrayed the shooting as another unprovoked attack by blacks on whites. The *Detroit Free Press* for September 10 included this description in its report:

Shots poured without warning and seemingly without provocation last night at 8:30 o'clock from the second-story windows of 2905 Garland Avenue into which Dr. and Mrs. Ossian Sweet, a Negro couple, had moved Tuesday, cost one man's life, put another in the hospital with a bullet in his leg, and called out 200 heavily armed police reserves, detectives, and regular policemen from every precinct, as well as an armored car. . . .

Leo Briener, 2906 Garland Avenue, father of two children, who was walking on the east side of Garland Avenue across the street from the house, was killed instantly, a bullet entering his head. Erik Halberg, 2910 Garland Avenue, 22 years old, ran out of his home when he heard the shooting and was just in time to receive one of the last bullets fired. He was taken to receiving hospital, shot in the leg. Briener was 33 years old. . . .

The *Detroit News* did not try quite so hard to portray the victims as innocent or unfortunate passersby:

> . . . Breiner was standing near the porch of the home of Ray Dove, 2914 Garland Avenue, talking to Dove and Hogberg. The two men fell at the first shots and others in the volley, which seemed directed at the Dove home, narrowly missed Mrs. Dove and her child, 20 months old, who were on the porch. . . .
>
> Breiner died as he was being carried to the hospital, and Hogberg, shot in the chest, is in a serious condition.

The *Free Press* and the *News* could not agree on the details of the shooting of the victims; where they were at the time, the nature of their wounds, or even the spelling of their names. There was, however, absolute agreement that the crowd had been peaceful, nonviolent, nonprovoking, and nonhostile. The authority cited by both papers was, of course, the Detroit Police Department.

V

The Confession

These men were taken to the police station. Gentlemen, there was never a time that these black men's rights were protected in the least; never once. They had no rights—they are black. They were to be driven out of their home, under the law's protection. When they defended their home, they were arrested and charged with murder. They were taken to a police station, manacled, and they asked for a lawyer. And, every man, if he has any brains at all, asks for a lawyer when he is in the hands of the police. If he does not want to have a web woven around him, to entangle or ensnare him, he will ask for a lawyer. And, the lawyer's first aid to the injured always is, "Keep your mouth shut." It is not a case of whether you are guilty or not guilty. That makes no difference. "Keep your mouth shut." The police grabbed them, as is their habit. They got the county attorney to ask questions. What did they do? They did what everybody does, helpless, alone and unadvised. They did not know, even, that anybody was killed. . . . But, they knew that they had been arrested for defending their own right to live; and they were in the hands of their enemies; and they told the best story they could think of at that time—just as ninety-nine men out of a hundred always do, whether they are guilty or not guilty makes no difference. But lawyers, and even policemen, should have protected their rights. Some things that these defendants said were not true, and as is

always the case. . . . These conflicting statements you
will find in all cases of this sort. You always find them
where men have been sweated, without help, without a
lawyer, groping around blindly, in the hands of the
enemy, without the aid of anybody to protect their rights.
Gentlemen, from the first to the last, there has not been
a substantial right of these defendants that was not
violated.

Leon Breiner and Erik Haugberg had been shot at 8:25 P.M.,
on September 9. But no one in the Sweet household knew
about that until they were told, at 3:30 A.M. on September 10,
by an assistant prosecutor, that he would recommend first-
degree murder warrants against all eleven. Up to that point,
none of the eleven had been told why they had been arrested.

After Ossian Sweet had assured Inspector Schuknecht that
there would be no more shooting, Schuknecht had left the
house, apparently satisfied. But moments later he had returned, this time with five other policemen. All eleven occupants were herded into the living room and handcuffed. A
search of the house quickly turned up the guns and ammunition, which, together with the prisoners, were loaded into
police vans and taken downtown. They were not, however,
told that anyone had been shot or why they were being
arrested.

Upon arrival at police headquarters, teams of officers began
separate interrogations of each defendant. This was almost
half a century before the Supreme Court of the United States,
in the *Escobedo* case, held that a person in custody has a
constitutional right to assistance of counsel before interrogation, and ruled, in the *Miranda* case, that prior to questioning,
a suspect must be advised of his right to remain silent, that
any statement he makes may be used as evidence against him,

and that he has the right to the presence of a lawyer, either retained by·him or furnished by the state.

The Detroit police were not about to afford any procedural safeguards that the law did not require, and though Ossian Sweet had demanded the right to call a lawyer immediately upon being arrested, this right was denied. Each defendant was intensively questioned for over six hours, without any warning whatsoever, till they were finally told that Leon Breiner had been killed and that each would be charged with first-degree murder.

The defendants told wildly disparate stories. Several claimed to have been sleeping at the time of the shooting, though it is doubtful that anyone had done any sleeping during the thirty-six hours that the Sweets had occupied the house. Several denied all knowledge of the existence of guns, though Ossian Sweet freely admitted that he had distributed a gun to each male except William Davis, who had his own. Joe Mack even claimed to have been taking a bath at the time of the shooting, which, if true, would have been a remarkable act of indifference to the howling mob outside. The only one who admitted firing any shots was Henry Sweet, who said he fired several shots in the air, just as a warning to the crowd.

Mrs. Sweet, who admitted to nothing more than having spent the entire evening in the kitchen cooking a ham for the men, was charged with murder along with the rest. As Arthur Garfield Hays, one of the defense counsel at the subsequent trial, was to remark—if the Sweets' baby daughter had been at home instead of two miles away with her grandmother, she no doubt would also have been arrested for murder.

It was not the first nor the last time that a basic principle of American law enforcement had been applied—if it appears that a crime has been committed, and if it is possible that a black man has committed it, arrest every black in sight.

PART II

VI

White Supremacy–
Supreme Court Style

He is black, partly black. What are you, gentlemen?
And what am I? I don't know. I can only go a little way
toward the source of my own being. I know my father
and I know my mother. I knew my grandmothers and my
grandfathers on both sides, but I didn't know my great-
grandfathers and great-grandmothers on either side, and
I don't know who they were. All that a man can do in
this direction is but little. He can only slightly raise the
veil that hangs over the past. . . .

I know that back of us all and each of us is the blood
of all the world. I know that it courses in your veins and
in mine, it has all come out of the infinite past, and I can't
pick out mine and you can't pick out yours, and it is only
the ignorant who know, and I believe that back of that
is what we call the lower order of life; back of that there
lurks the instinct of the distant serpent, of the carnivorous
tiger. All the elements have been gathered together to
make the mixture that is you and I and all the race,
and nobody knows anything about his own. Gentlemen,
I wonder who we are anyhow to be so proud about our
ancestry? We had better try to do something to be proud
of ourselves; we had better try to do something kindly,
something humane, to some human being, than to brag
about our ancestry, of which none of us know anything.

The function of bail in a criminal case is to insure the presence of the defendant for trial. Excessive bail is, in fact, prohibited by the Eighth Amendment in the Bill of Rights. Holding a criminal defendant without bail would appear to be as excessive as it is possible to be, but the Eighth Amendment has never been construed to require bail in all cases.

There seemed to be little or no risk that any of the Sweet case defendants would flee the jurisdiction. All were longtime residents of Detroit. Leonard Morris, Morris Murray, Hewitt Watson, Ossian Sweet, and Charles Washington had wives and children in the city. Ossian Sweet, of course, had his medical practice there and Otis Sweet his dental practice.

None of the defendants had ever been convicted of a crime and there was no record that any of them, prior to September 9, 1925, had ever been arrested. The military careers of Otis Sweet and William Davis in World War I and Davis' experience as a federal narcotics agent were as close to guns and violence as any of the defendants had ever been.

If the question of bail were to be considered on the basis of the usual criteria, then there could be little doubt that these defendants were entitled to bail. But Judge John Faust, not willing to risk the reaction of white Detroit, incensed by the killing, denied bail when the firm of Rowlette, Perry, and Mahoney, Negro attorneys who had been retained by Mrs. Mitchell, Gladys Sweet's mother, applied in behalf of all the defendants.

Following the preliminary hearing before Judge Faust on September 16, Judge Frank Murphy, presiding judge of the Recorders Court, exercising his prerogative as presiding judge, assigned himself to the trial of the Sweet case and Cecil Rowlette decided to renew his motion for bail. He had reason to hope that Judge Murphy would be more sympathetic toward his clients. Murphy, thirty-five years old, had acquired a reputation as a liberal judge and a friend of Detroit's black community, based largely on the bitter opposition to him by the Ku Klux Klan. Hatred of the Klan would at least give the defendants something in common with the judge.

Murphy was, in fact, considered to be one of Detroit's most promising public figures and later he more than fulfilled that promise. He was aware that his career could be given some impetus by his participation in the Sweet case though he claimed that he took the case only because no other judge would.

> . . . Every Judge on this bench is afraid. . . . They think it's dynamite. They don't realize that this is the opportunity of a lifetime to demonstrate sincere liberalism and judicial integrity at a time when liberalism is coming into its own.

That the case was an opportunity for a judge is without question. That the other judges were unwilling to take the case is doubtful. Judges are not notorious for shying away from publicity-prone cases. The liberalism displayed by Judge Murphy in the Sweet trials does not seem remarkable from this distance, but he later firmly established his credentials as a progressive and fearless public servant. The Detroit Recorders Court was not nearly large enough to hold his talents. In 1930 he was elected mayor of Detroit and starting in 1933 he became one of President Roosevelt's favorite appointees—first as governor general of the Philippines, then as high commissioner to the Philippines in 1935. In 1937, he was elected governor of Michigan and in 1939, FDR made him attorney general of the United States. This spectacular career was capped by his appointment, in 1941, as a justice of the United States Supreme Court, where he served with distinction until his death in 1949.

His finest hour came in 1944, when he dissented from the Supreme Court's opinion upholding the action of the United States government in what must be considered one of its darkest hours. This country has always been at its worst in dealing with problems of race. The treatment of the red man and the black man had apparently not exhausted the seemingly bottomless reservoir of racial hatred and fear—after Pearl Harbor the American yellow man had his turn. With the same kind of panic and unreasoning hysteria that had characterized the waterworks improvers in 1925, the government of the United States, in 1942, institutionalized racism against Japanese-Americans.

Shortly after Pearl Harbor, under the war powers granted to him by Congress, the President had issued Executive Order No. 59066 which declared that:

> The successful prosecution of the war requires every possible protection against espionage and against sabotage to national defense material, national defense premises, and national defense utilities. . . .

Give a military commander a Gulf of Tonkin and he will take a mile, so immediately upon the issuance of this executive order the Western Command saw sabotage and espionage in every yellow face and began issuing a series of military orders chipping away at the rights of Japanese-Americans. First came an order establishing a curfew in certain designated military zones, encompassing entire cities, prohibiting the presence of Italian aliens, German aliens, and persons of Japanese ancestry, whether alien or not, within the hours of 8:00 P.M. and 6:00 A.M.

The military zones were gradually increased and finally the commanding general of the Western Military Command in May, 1942, set in motion the machinery for the final solution of the Japanese problem, which was to be the forcible evacuation and relocation of all Japanese from the entire West Coast and a large part of Arizona. This outrageous order, which was duly approved all the way up to the highest military and civilian levels, including the White House, meant that 112,000 Japanese-Americans, 70,000 of them native-born citizens, were to be uprooted from their homes, deprived of much of their property, and placed in inland detention camps—

solely on the basis of "Japanese ancestry," without any showing of individual disloyalty, without hearing, without appeal,
and without hope, even from the Supreme Court of the United
States, which upheld the action.

It is extremely ironic that the Supreme Court, which in the
last two decades, often in defiance of the other branches of
government, has valiantly, if futilely, tried to redress so many
racial wrongs, was responsible in the first instance for turning
the country in the wrong direction each time there was an
opportunity to make a fresh start in race relations. In three
Supreme Court decisions the country made the fatal choices
that were to give the majesty of law to racial attitudes which
have brought us directly to where we are today. The first of
these landmark cases was the *Dred Scott* decision in 1857.
Dred Scott had been the slave of a Missouri doctor who had
taken Scott to live in the free state of Illinois, and in that part
of the Missouri territory, later the state of Minnesota, in which
slavery had been abolished by the Missouri Compromise. Upon
returning to Missouri, a slave state, the doctor sold Scott to a
New Yorker named John Sanford, who presumably had some
use for a slave in Missouri. Encouraged by abolitionists who
told him that his residence in free territory had made him a
free man, Scott sued Sanford for freedom for himself, his
wife, and his children (Sanford owned them all) in the federal court in Missouri. Chief Justice Taney in his opinion said:

> The question is simply this: Can a Negro, whose ances-
> tors were imported into this country and sold as slaves,
> become a member of the political community formed
> and brought into existence by the Constitution of the
> United States, and as such become entitled to all the
> rights, and privileges, and immunities, guaranteed by
> that instrument to the citizens.

Taney's answer, simply, was no, and his reasoning was that
the founding fathers had considered blacks to be inferior
beings and had said as much when the nation was formed.
It was as though he were saying that if God had wanted blacks

to be free he would have said so in the Declaration of Independence and the Constitution:

> It is difficult at this day to realize the state of public opinion in relation to that unfortunate race, which prevailed in the civilized and enlightened portions of the world at the time of the Declaration of Independence, and when the Constitution of the United States was formed and adopted. . . . They had for more than a century before been regarded as beings of an inferior order; and altogether unfit to associate with the white race, either in social or political relations; and so far inferior, that they had no rights which the white man was bound to respect; and that the Negro might justly and lawfully be reduced to slavery for his benefit. He was bought and sold, and treated as an ordinary article of merchandise and traffic whenever a profit could be made by it. This opinion was at that time fixed and universal in the civilized portion of the white race. It was regarded as an axiom in morals as well as in politics, which no one thought of disputing, or supposed to be open to dispute; and men in every grade and position in society daily and habitually acted upon it in their private pursuits, as well as in matters of public concern, without doubting for a moment the correctness of this opinion.

Taney then went on to say that although the Constitution does not specifically grant or deny citizenship to blacks, although, in fact, the Declaration of Independence did not exclude them when it said "all men are created equal," a strict construction of the Constitution at the time of its adoption nevertheless required the conclusion that a black could not become a citizen, whether free or not, and that therefore Scott had no standing to sue in federal court. The practical effect of this ruling was that Scott and his family remained the property of John Sanford, the absentee owner in New York.

It was not, explained Taney, that civilized society still

entertained such a mean opinion of the black race, but that the Constitution simply compelled the decision (two members of the Court and much of the population of the country were convinced that it did not).

> No one, we presume, supposes that any change in public opinion or feeling in relation to this unfortunate race . . . should induce the court to give to the words of the Constitution a more liberal construction in their favor than they were intended to bear when the instrument was framed and adopted. . . . If any of its provisions are deemed unjust, there is a mode prescribed in the instrument itself by which it may be amended; but while it remains unaltered, it must be construed now as it was understood at the time of its adoption.

In other words, this is the way it is with us whites and you blacks and this is the way it will be until us whites change it. Though the decision did not make Scott free, it made him famous, and shortly after the opinion was handed down he and his family were manumitted. He became a porter in a St. Louis hotel.

Thirty years later, the Supreme Court apparently was still determined to find no comfort in the Constitution for "this unfortunate race." Following the Civil War the reconstruction Congress had passed a sweeping and promising Civil Rights Act guaranteeing "full and equal enjoyment of the accommodations, advantages, facilities, and privileges of inns, public conveyances on land or water, theatres, and other places of public amusements . . ." and providing civil and criminal penalties for the denial of such rights.

The Thirteenth Amendment had abolished slavery and the Fourteenth had finally made citizens of blacks and had granted them the equal protection of the laws, or so it was thought, and when the constitutional challenge to the 1866 Civil Rights Act reached the Supreme Court in 1883 it was defended on the basis of those amendments. By then reconstruction was dead, killed by shabby political deals, much as the second reconstruction of the post–World War II era was killed by "southern strategy." It remained for the Supreme Court to nail down the coffin. It struck down the Civil Rights Act and remanded blacks for the protection of those rights to the mercy of those states abiding by the black codes which Congress, before its reformist zeal died, had tried to abolish.

> When a man has emerged from slavery [said the Court], and by the aid of beneficial legislation has shaken off the inseparable concomitants of that state, there must be some stage in the progress of his elevation when he takes the rank of a mere citizen, and ceases to be the special favorite of the laws, and when his rights as a citizen or man, are to be protected in the ordinary modes by which other men's rights are protected. There were thousands of free colored people in this country before the abolition of slavery, enjoying all the essential rights of life, liberty, and property the same as white citizens; yet no one, at that time, thought that it was any invasion of their personal status as free men because they were not admitted to all the privileges enjoyed by white citizens, or because they were subjected to discrimination in the enjoyment of accommodations in inns, public conveyances and places of amusement. Mere discriminations on account of race or color were not regarded as badges of slavery.

There it was, way back in 1883. ". . . There must be some stage . . . when he takes the rank of a mere citizen, and ceases to be the special favorite of the laws. . . ." What do these people want, anyway? After all, the only thing involved here was "mere discriminations on account of race or color. . . ."

That the result in the Civil Rights cases was not constitutionally required is made clear by the dissent of Justice John Marshall Harlan, the grandfather of the present Justice Harlan. He wrote:

> . . . If the grant to colored citizens of the United States of citizenship in their respective states, imports exemp-

tions from race discrimination, in their states, in respect
of such civil rights as belong to citizenship, then, to
hold that amendment remits that right to the states for
their protection, primarily, and stays the hand of the
nation, until it is assailed by state laws or state proceedings, is to adjudge that the amendment, so far from
enlarging the powers of Congress as we have heretofore
said it did, not only curtails them, but reverses the
policy which the general government had pursued from
its very organization . . . would lead to this anomalous
result: That whereas, prior to the amendments, Congress, with the sanction of this Court, passed the most
stringent laws—operating directly and primarily upon
states and their officers and agents, as well as upon the
individuals—in vindication of slavery and the right of
the master, it may not now, by legislation of a like
primary and direct character, guard, protect, and secure
the freedom established, and the most essential right
of the citizenship granted, by the constitutional amendments. . . .

What Justice Harlan was saying, in the sometimes obscure
manner of justices, was that though this country had been
willing to use the national machinery of its legislative and
legal system for the protection and perpetuation of slavery
and repression, it had abandoned its national commitment to
freedom.

If Justice Harlan was unhappy with the majority opinion in
the Civil Rights cases, he was to be near despair when the
Court took its next giant step backwards in *Plessy* v. *Ferguson*
twenty years later. The Court in the Civil Rights cases had
held only that Congress did not have the power to adopt equal
accommodation laws and that the Thirteenth and Fourteenth
Amendments were meant to serve solely as protection against
discriminatory state action, as distinguished from individual
action. The states were quick to realize that though the Fourteenth Amendment had made blacks citizens, the national

policy elected to establish a second-class citizenship. Accordingly, Jim Crow became the law of the land. In 1896, the country was given another chance to wipe the slate clean and start the new century with a commitment to democratic ideals, but it chose instead to look backward into the nineteenth century. On June 7, 1892, a New Orleans man named Homer Adolph Plessy bought a train ticket and rode into history. Plessy claimed that since seven of his eight immediate forebears were white and only one was black, he should be entitled to sit in the "white only" car of a Louisiana train. He, in fact, appeared to be white, but Southern train conductors were notoriously sharp-eyed in spotting black blood, and when Plessy refused to move into the black coach, he was taken off the train and arrested. His conviction under Louisiana's separate but equal statute finally reached the Supreme Court with Plessy's contention that the statute was unconstitutional and that in any case he hadn't violated it since he was more white than black. (An ominous portent of the twentieth century lay in that argument. Nazi Germany, the Union of South Africa, and the United States of America all developed complex bodies of law dealing with subtle distinctions of racial purity. Some nice physical, if not metaphysical, questions might have been posed for the learned justices if Plessy had been a little more imaginative, not to say acrobatic, and had stationed seven-eighths of himself in the white coach with perhaps one leg extending into the black coach.)

The Court had no difficulty in upholding the constitutionality of the statute:

> So far, then, as a conflict with the Fourteenth Amendment is concerned, the case reduces itself to the question whether the statute of Louisiana is a reasonable regulation. . . .
>
> In determining the question of reasonableness it is at liberty to act with reference to the established usages, customs, and traditions of the people, and with a view to the promotion of their comfort, and the preservation

of the public peace and good order. Gauged by this standard, we cannot say that a law which authorizes or even requires the separation of the two races in public conveyances is unreasonable, or more obnoxious to the Fourteenth Amendment than the acts of Congress requiring separate schools for colored children in the District of Columbia, the constitutionality of which does not seem to have been questioned, or the corresponding acts of state legislatures.

This was typical of the dreary history of white America's rationale of race relations—using one wrong as justification for another. The Court continued:

We consider the underlying fallacy of the Plaintiff's argument to consist in the assumption that the enforced separation of the two races stamps the colored race with a badge of inferiority. If this be so, it is not by reason of anything found in the act, but solely because the colored race chooses to put that construction upon it. The argument necessarily assumes that if, as has been more than once the case, and is not unlikely to be so again, the colored race should become the dominant power in the state legislature, and should enact a law in precisely similar terms, it would thereby relegate the white race to an inferior position. We imagine that the white race, at least, would not acquiesce in this assumption.

Translation: blacks are inferior to whites, and whites, at least, are certain of this and so it is silly to even hypothesize differently. This inferiority was an article of faith to the Court which reiterated its belief: "If one race be inferior to the other socially, the Constitution of the United States cannot put them in the same place." The Court then went on to assert that the statute was not discriminatory since, just as blacks were prohibited from riding in white cars, whites were prohibited from riding in black cars. In America, as in Paris, it is as illegal for the rich as for the poor to sleep under bridges.

Finally, the Court addressed itself briefly to the question: what is a Negro? and then begged it:

> It is true that the question of the proportion of colored blood necessary to constitute a colored person, as distinguished from a white person, is one upon which there is a difference of opinion in the different states; some holding that any visible admixture of black blood stamps the person as belonging to the colored race . . . others that it depends upon the preponderance of blood . . . and still others, that the predominance of white blood must only be in the proportion of three-fourths. . . . But these questions are to be determined under the laws of each state.

(In 1970 the state of Louisiana was still wrestling with this knotty problem. Its House of Representatives passed a bill clarifying the official definition of a Negro in Louisiana. The bill states:

> In signifying race, a person having one thirty-second or less of Negro blood shall not be deemed, described or designated by any public official of the state of Louisiana as "colored," a "mulatto," a "black," a "Negro," a "griff," an "Afro-American," a "quadroon," a "mestizo," a "colored person," or a "person of color.")

Justice Harlan, in perhaps as prophetic a dissent as has ever been written by a Supreme Court justice, warned that this country would rue the day that its highest court indelibly stamped ten million of its citizens as inferior:

> In my opinion, the judgment this day rendered will, in time, prove to be quite as pernicious as the decision made by this tribunal in the *Dred Scott* case. . . .
> The arbitrary separation of citizens, on the basis of race, while they are on a public highway, is a badge of

servitude wholly inconsistent with the civil freedom and the equality before the law established by the Constitution. It cannot be justified upon any legal grounds. . . .

We boast of the freedom enjoyed by our people above all other peoples. But it is difficult to reconcile that boast with a state of the law which, practically, puts the brand of servitude and degradation upon a large class of our fellow citizens—our equals before the law. The thin disguise of "equal" accommodations for passengers in railroad coaches will not mislead anyone, nor atone for the wrong this day done.

The justice almost seemed to be advising civil disobedience:

It is scarcely just to say that a colored citizen should not object to occupying a public coach assigned to his own race. . . . But he does object, and he ought never to cease objecting, that citizens of the white and black races can be adjudged criminals because they sit, or claim the right to sit, in the same public coach on a public highway.

Finally, Justice Harlan expressed his view that this insidious opinion which elevated racism to the level of a constitutional imperative, and perhaps foreclosed forever the prospect of racial harmony in America, was in no respect required by logic, precedent, or indeed, by strict constitutional construction:

I do not deem it necessary to review the decisions of state courts to which reference was made in argument. Some, and the most important, of them are wholly inapplicable because rendered prior to the adoption of the last amendments of the Constitution, when colored people had very few rights which the dominant race felt obliged to respect. Others were made at a time when public opinion, in many localities, was dominated by the institution of slavery; when, so far as the rights of blacks were concerned, race prejudice was, practically, the supreme law of the land.

These decisions cannot be guides in the era introduced by the recent amendments of the Supreme Law, which established universal civil rights, gave citizenship to all born or naturalized in the United States, and residing here, obliterated the race line, from our systems of governments, national and state, and placed our free institutions upon the broad and sure foundation of the equality of all men before the law.

This country is now reaping the bitter harvest of the separate but equal seed planted by *Plessy* v. *Ferguson* which remained the supreme law of the land for half a century and which has led directly to what the Kerner Commission has called two nations—one white, and one black, and both armed. Small wonder that the residents of Garland and Charlevoix rebelled in 1925 at the thought of a black family in their midst. These were inferior people. The leaders of their country—the executive, the legislative, and the judicial—had constantly told them so. It was their right, and possibly their duty, to drive these black invaders from the neighborhood.

The doctrine of white supremacy according to the Supreme Court was restated in 1944 in the decision upholding the constitutionality of the Japanese evacuation orders. Anyone who considers it impossible that the United States government would ever place blacks in detention camps if, in the view of the administration, they became too threatening though free of criminal action, is advised to regard carefully the *Korematsu* case, substituting for the military views referred to in the opinion, certain pronouncements of the current vice-president and the attorney general of the United States, not to mention the director of the Federal Bureau of Investigation. These advocates of law and order, who seem to believe that the answer to crime in the streets lies in preventive detention, hold the loaded gun that Justice Robert Jackson referred to in his dissenting opinion in the *Korematsu* case:

. . . The court for all time has validated the principle of racial discrimination in criminal procedure and of transplanting American citizens. The principle then lies about like a loaded weapon ready for the hand of any authority that can bring forward a plausible claim of an urgent need.

Fred Korematsu, an American citizen and lifelong resident of California who had not been charged with any act of disloyalty, had refused to leave his home in San Leandro to report to an assembly center for eventual relocation. A six-man majority of the United States Supreme Court, including men generally considered to be as good as our judicial system can produce—Chief Justice Harlan Fiske Stone, Justice Hugo Black, Justice Felix Frankfurter, and Justice William O. Douglas—not a Carswell or a Haynsworth in the lot—affirmed the conviction of Korematsu. The majority opinion is an abject surrender to the military mind:

> Like curfew, exclusion of those of Japanese origin was deemed necessary because of the presence of an unascertained number of disloyal members of the group, most of whom we have no doubt were loyal to this country. It was because we could not reject the finding of the military authorities that it was impossible to bring about an immediate segregation of the disloyal from the loyal that we sustained the validity of the curfew order as applying to the whole group. In the instant case, temporary exclusion of the group was rested by the military on the same ground. The judgment that exclusion of the whole group was for the same reason a military necessity answers the contention that the exclusion was in the nature of group punishment based on antagonism to those of Japanese origin.

The Court then resorted to a "war is hell" argument:

> We uphold the exclusion order. . . . In doing so, we are not unmindful of the hardships imposed by it, upon a

large number of American citizens. But hardships are part of war, and war is an aggregation of hardships. All citizens alike, both in and out of uniform, feel the impact of war in greater or lesser measure.

And, finally, the Court, not insensitive to the outrage it was condoning, tried to convince itself that it was not really doing what it was doing:

It is said that we are dealing here with the case of imprisonment of a citizen in a concentration camp solely because of his ancestry, without evidence or inquiry concerning his loyalty and good disposition towards the United States. . . .

Regardless of the true nature of the assembly and relocation centers—and we deem it unjustifiable to call them concentration camps with all the ugly connotations that term implies—we are dealing specifically with nothing but an exclusion order. To cast this case into outlines of racial prejudice without reference to the real military dangers which were presented, merely confuses the issue. Korematsu was not excluded from the military area because of hostility to him or his race. He was excluded because we are at war with the Japanese Empire, because the properly constituted military authorities feared an invasion of our West Coast and felt constrained to take proper security measures, because they decided that the military urgency of the situation demanded that all citizens of Japanese ancestry be segregated from the West Coast temporarily, and finally, because Congress, reposing its confidence in this time of war in our military leaders, as inevitably it must, determined that they should have the power to do just this.

Accepting the military judgment, as the Court did, is to agree with another old military judgment that the only good Indian is a dead Indian. Regardless of the Court's disclaimer, the net result of the action taken was a displacement of over

70,000 citizens and 40,000 resident aliens solely because of race. This country was also at war with Germany and with Italy and in fact the military had more reason to fear attacks on the East Coast than on the West. A German submarine had, two years earlier, landed nine German saboteurs off Long Island and Florida. But Germans and Italians are white and the military did not for a moment consider the relocation of Germans and Italians, whether citizens or aliens, from any part of the country.

Justice Frank Murphy had had enough. He dissented from the majority opinion along with Justice Roberts and Justice Jackson. Murphy had reluctantly agreed with the majority in 1943 in upholding the curfew regulations in the *Hirabayashi* case. In a concurring opinion he had expressed grave doubt that military danger, real or imagined, should justify such a radical infringement on freedom:

> Today is the first time, as far as I am aware, that we have sustained a substantial restriction on the personal liberty of citizens of the United States based upon the accident of race or ancestry. [It was not the first time.] Under the curfew order here challenged no less than 70,000 American citizens have been placed under a special ban and deprived of their liberty because of their particular racial inheritance. In this sense it bears a melancholy resemblance to the treatment accorded to members of the Jewish race in Germany and in other parts of Europe. The result is the creation in this country of two classes of citizens for the purpose of a critical and perilous hour—to sanction discrimination between groups of United States citizens on the basis of ancestry. In my opinion this goes to the very brink of Constitutional power.

(By 1944 the country had become so accustomed to the two classes of citizens created by *Plessy* v. *Ferguson* that Justice Murphy was able to consider the dichotomy unique in the Japanese evacuation cases.)

Murphy made it clear that he would have considered the curfew beyond the brink of Constitutional power had it not been justified as a temporary emergency, and had he not assumed that the military would go no further in the restriction of the liberties of innocent citizens on a discriminatory basis.

But the military always goes further and though Murphy, in the earlier case, had accepted a temporary curfew, he would not accept evacuation and relocation. The American racial sickness that Judge Murphy of the Recorders Court saw in the Sweet Case in 1925 is echoed in the dissenting opinion of Justice Murphy in 1944 in the *Korematsu* case:

This exclusion of "all persons of Japanese ancestry, both alien and nonalien" from the Pacific Coast area on a plea of military necessity in the absence of martial law ought not to be approved. Such exclusion goes over "the very brink of Constitutional power" and falls into the ugly abyss of racism. . . .

That this forced exclusion was the result in good measure of this erroneous assumption of racial guilt rather than bona fide military necessity is evidenced by the Commanding General's Final Report on the Evacuation of the Pacific Coast Area. In it he refers to all individuals of Japanese descent as "subversive," as belonging to "an enemy race" whose racial strains are "undiluted." . . .

In support of this blanket condemnation of all persons of Japanese descent, however, no reliable evidence is cited to show that such individuals were generally disloyal. . . .

Justification for the exclusion is sought, instead, mainly upon questionable racial and sociological grounds not ordinarily within the realm of expert military judgment. . . .

The reasons appear, instead, to be largely an accumulation of much of the misinformation, half-truths and insinuations that for years have been directed against

Japanese-Americans by people with racial and economic prejudices—the same people who have been among the foremost advocates of the evacuation. . . .

But, to infer that examples of individual disloyalty prove group disloyalty and justify discriminatory action against the entire group is to deny that under our system of law individual guilt is the sole basis for deprivation of rights. . . .

No adequate reason is given for the failure to treat these Japanese-Americans on an individual basis by holding investigations and hearings to separate the loyal from the disloyal, as was done in the case of persons of German and Italian ancestry. . . .

I dissent, therefore, from this legalization of racism. Social discrimination in any form and in any degree has no justifiable part whatever in our democratic way of life. It is unattractive in any setting but it is utterly revolting among a free people who have embraced the principles set forth in the Constitution of the United States. All residents of this nation are kin in some way by blood or culture to a foreign land. Yet they are primarily and necessarily a part of the new and distinct civilization of the United States. They must accordingly be treated at all times as the heirs of the American experiment and are entitled to all the rights and freedoms guaranteed by the Constitution.

It is, perhaps, a romantic notion to think that Frank Murphy in 1944 was saying some things about race in America which he would have wanted to say in Detroit in 1925. But in 1925 the ambitious politician in Frank Murphy dominated the liberal jurist and the most he would risk on October 2 in ruling on Rowlette's motion for bail was to release Gladys Sweet on $5,000 bail and deny the motion as to the others. Even this innocuous act brought a severe reaction from white Detroiters and Judge Murphy was accused of turning a vengeful black loose upon a defenseless community. But Mrs. Sweet, whose only weapon had been the never-eaten ham, devoted her freedom to taking care of her child and visiting her husband, his brothers, and friends in the Wayne County Jail. With Detroit in a state of near panic and with newspaper comments like "cold-blooded murder," "another murder by Negroes," "they are becoming a menace to the country," and "race war killing," it is not surprising that Judge Murphy, on October 13, overruled Rowlette's motion to quash the indictment and discharge the defendants.

The motion had merit and in a less hysterical atmosphere might have been granted. Rowlette argued that the evidence at the preliminary hearing had fallen far short of showing probable cause that the defendants, either jointly or severally, had killed Leon Breiner. The Michigan first-degree murder statute read as follows:

> All murder which shall be perpetrated by means of poison or by lying in wait, or any other kind of willful, deliberate and premeditated killing; or which shall be committed in the perpetration or attempt to perpetrate any arson, rape, robbery or burglary shall be deemed murder in the first degree and shall be punished in the State Prison for life.

Rowlette argued that under this statute it was necessary to determine which defendant fired the shot that killed Breiner and that he or she alone could be prosecuted. He claimed that there had been no evidence as to which, if any, of the defendants had fired the fatal shot, or even that the shot which killed Breiner had come from the Sweet house. Judge Murphy was not willing to substitute himself as the object of the white community's vengeance. The motion was denied as to all defendants and they were ordered to stand trial commencing October 30.

PART III

VII

John Brown's Body

Gentlemen, nature works in a queer way. I don't know how this question of color will ever be solved, or whether it will be solved. I look on a trial like this with a feeling of disgust and shame. I can't help it now. It will be after we have learned in the terrible and expensive school of human experience that we will be willing to find each other and understand each other. . . .

If the race that we belong to owes anything to any human being, or any power in this universe, they owe it to these black men. Above all other men, they owe an obligation and a duty to these black men which can never be repaid. I never see one of them, that I do not feel I ought to pay part of the debt of my race,—and if you gentlemen feel as you should feel in this case, your emotions will be like mine.

A more than casual observer of the preliminary procedure had been Walter H. White, the assistant secretary of the National Association for the Advancement of Colored People. The NAACP, since its founding in 1909, had been the most active and prestigious black organization in the country. But since the new black militancy of the postwar years, it had been

under increasing criticism from other black organizations for
an alleged lack of aggressiveness and an overinvolvement with
white people.

This attitude was becoming more prevalent in spite of the
fact that W. E. B. Du Bois, one of the organization's founders
and the editor of its publication, *Crisis*, was one of the most
militant black leaders in the country, and often predicted
open warfare between blacks and whites. He had, in fact,
written that World War I was "nothing to compare with that
fight for freedom which black and brown and yellow men
must and will make unless their oppression and humiliation
and insult at the hands of the white world cease."

To Du Bois the militancy of Ossian Sweet was precisely that
fight against oppression, humiliation, and insult, and he determined to involve the NAACP in the case. In the first issue of
Crisis following the shooting he wrote:

> In Detroit, Michigan, a black man has shot into a mob
> which was threatening him, his family, his friends, and
> his home in order to make him move out of the neigh-
> borhood. He killed one man and wounded another.
>
> Immediately, a red and awful challenge confronts the
> nation. Must black folk shoot and shoot to kill in order
> to maintain their rights or is this unnecessary and wan-
> ton bloodshed for fancied ill? . . . The mayor of Detroit
> has publicly warned both mob and Negroes. He has
> repudiated mob law but he adds, turning to his darker
> audience, that they ought not to invite aggression by
> going where they are not wanted. . . .
>
> Dear God! Must we not live! And if we live may we
> not just live somewhere? And when a whole city full of
> white folk led and helped by banks, chambers of com-
> merce, mortgage companies, and "realtors" are combing
> the earth for every decent bit of residential property for
> whites, where in the name of God can we live and live
> decently if not by these same whites? If some of the
> horror-struck and law-worshiping white leaders of

Detroit, instead of winking at the Ku Klux Klan and admonishing the Negroes to allow themselves to be kicked and killed with impunity—if these would finance and administer a decent scheme of housing relief for Negroes it would not be necessary for us to kill white mob leaders in order to live in peace and decency. These whited sepulchers pulled that trigger and not the man that held the gun.

Walter White and James Weldon Johnson, the executive secretary of the NAACP, were interested in the Sweet case for more legalistic reasons. For several years they had led their organization in a broad-scale attack on various forms of housing segregation. The NAACP appeal to the United States Supreme Court in 1917 had been successful in striking down a Louisville, Kentucky, housing ordinance limiting the areas available for residency by blacks. They were, at the time of the Sweet case, engaged in attacking a similar statute in New Orleans. Also, winding its way slowly through the judicial process, was an NAACP challenge to restrictive covenants, a segregated housing device in which a condition of ownership of the property was a promise, deemed to "run with the land," to restrict future sales of the property to whites only.

The year 1925 saw an alarming rise throughout the country of segregation by violence and terror, and the Sweet case offered a perfect opportunity to strike a legal blow on behalf of the right of self-defense against such tactics. Walter White had not been overly impressed with the Detroit lawyers Mrs. Mitchell had hired. When he returned to New York he recommended that the NAACP retain additional counsel to appear with the local counsel on behalf of all the defendants. White thought a nationally known white attorney might offset some of the hostility to blacks which had been so obvious to him in Detroit. This suggestion at first met strong opposition from others in the organization and from Cecil Rowlette, who was heading the Detroit team of lawyers. As trial strategy, a white attorney would almost surely be a plus but, it was argued, the NAACP would subject itself to still more criticism from those complaining of white influence in the organization. The rising tide of black awareness and black self-reliance almost required that the trial team be headed by a black attorney.

But Walter White had not recommended a lawyer solely for the color of his skin. The man he urged the organization to retain was Clarence Darrow and there was no black or white lawyer in the country who could match Darrow in a courtroom. W. E. B. Du Bois, who yielded to no one in black militancy, ordinarily would have sided with those urging that a black lawyer be hired, but when he learned that Darrow might be persuaded to take the case, he immediately joined White in his recommendation. Du Bois had long known and liked Darrow. He had written:

> Being a Negro and rather tense in my feelings, I was drawn to Clarence Darrow because he was absolutely lacking in racial consciousness and because of the broad catholicity of his knowledge and tastes. He was one of the few white folk with whom I felt quite free to discuss matters of race and class which I usually would not bring up.

Du Bois went on to say that there was a looseness about Darrow much like the looseness of a freed slave in a story that Du Bois had heard Darrow tell on more than one occasion:

> "Sam, how are you getting on?"
> "Well, not doing so well."
> "Don't get food so regular as you used to?"
> "No, suh."
> "Don't have nobody to look after you?"
> "No, suh, that is a fact."
> "Well, Sam, weren't you better off in slavery?"
> "Well, I tells you, suh, it's like this: There's a sort of looseness about this here freedom that I likes."

Aside from his personal fondness for Darrow, there were many reasons why Du Bois should want him for the Sweet case. He was, without a doubt, the best criminal lawyer in the country; he was a long-time member and supporter of the NAACP; he was a genuine radical like Du Bois himself, and, perhaps most importantly, he had just finished the Scopes trial in Tennessee. Du Bois felt that ignorance lay at the root of America's racial problem and that Darrow could attack that ignorance in the Sweet case as he had attacked the ignorance that produced the Tennessee law that made it a crime to teach evolution in Tennessee schools.

Du Bois had written about the Scopes case:

One-hundred-percent-Americans are now endeavoring to persuade hilarious and sarcastic Europe that Dayton, Tennessee, is a huge joke and very very exceptional. And in proof of all this the learned American press is emitting huge guffaws and peals of Brobdingnagian laughter combined with streaming tears. But few are deceived, even of those who joke and slap each other on the back. The truth is and we know it: Dayton, Tennessee, is America! A great, ignorant, simple-minded land, curiously compounded of brutality, bigotry, religious faith and demagoguery, and capable not simply of mistakes but persecution, lynching, murder and idiotic blundering, as well as charity, missions, love and hope.

That is America and America is what it is because we believe in ignorance. The whole modern Nordic civilization of which America is a great and leading branch has sold its soul to ignorance. Its leading priests profess a religious faith which they do not believe and which they know, and every man of intelligence knows, they do not and cannot believe; and then when a knot of backwoodsmen led by some cheap demagogues try to drive out error in a logical way they learn to their own intense surprise that what the world was thinking and doing had in some unaccountable way been kept from them. Either, then, they have been deceived or are being attacked. They resent it and with the proper demagogue to lead they are ready to drive out heretics and defend the truth as they have received it with guns and fagots.

Who is to blame? They that know; they that teach; they that have; they that sit silent and enjoy; great universities that close their doors to the mob; great scientists who prostitute truth to prejudice; great preachers who quibble with faith and facts; great rulers of wealth who fear understanding; and voluptuaries who have no wish to be disturbed by real democracy.

The folk who leave white Tennessee in blank and ridiculous ignorance of what science has taught the world since 1859 are the same ones who would leave black Tennessee and black America with just as little education as is consistent with fairly efficient labor and reasonable contentment; who rave over the Eighteenth Amendment and are dumb over the Fifteenth; who permit lynching and make bastardy legal in order to render their race "pure." It is such folk who, when in sudden darkness they descry the awful faces of the Fanatic, the Fury and the Fool, try to hide the vision with gales of laughter.

But, Dayton, Tennessee, is no laughing matter. It is menace and warning. It is a challenge to Religion, Science and Democracy.

(In 1925, at the time of the Scopes trial, the state of Mississippi adopted an antievolution teaching law. In January, 1970, the Mississippi House of Representatives voted 70–42 against a bill to repeal the statute. The representative leading the fight to retain the law which makes it a crime to teach evolution in Mississippi schools said, "If this law is going to be repealed, let it be done by a federal judge, not by the people of this State, because we need all the divine help we can get.

These are Christian statutes on our books, and I believe Christians are still in control of this State.")

Ignorance was the enemy. In order to defend the Sweets, it would be necessary to attack ignorance. There was no doubt in Du Bois' mind that Clarence Darrow was the best man for both jobs.

At the time of Ossian Smith's arrest, Clarence Darrow, who had been born and raised in rural Ohio, maintained his office in Chicago, but practiced throughout the country, was visiting his friend Arthur Garfield Hays in New York. Hays, a forty-four-year-old lawyer, had been general counsel of the American Civil Liberties Union since 1922. He and Darrow had been together in the Scopes trial, an association that started a close friendship which lasted till Darrow's death in 1938. Darrow was sixty-eight and tired. The Scopes trial had only recently been completed in the oppressive heat of an overcrowded, hostility-filled courtroom in Dayton, Tennessee. The trial in fact had been so arduous that it had probably killed William Jennings Bryan, who had been Darrow's adversary as special prosecutor for the state of Tennessee. Bryan, who was sixty-five, collapsed two days after the trial and died in Dayton.

The previous year, 1924, had been just as strenuous for Darrow. He had spent most of it on the defense of Richard Loeb and Nathan Leopold, Jr., in Chicago, and had performed a minor miracle by saving them from the gallows. But it had been an emotionally exhausting experience. It had been a particularly abhorrent crime; he found it hard to sympathize with his clients, and he found them difficult to handle. And finally, after he had saved them from the death penalty, which was what he had been retained to do, their very wealthy parents paid him only one-third of the fee which they had promised. Ordinarily he would not take a case unless he liked the client or the cause and there was nothing about either that attracted him in Loeb–Leopold. (He did, of course, use the case as a platform for an attack on capital punishment, but he had done that many times before.) He did not often have clients who could afford such fees, but when the killers' parents offered him only $30,000 instead of the agreed-upon $100,000 he was too tired and disgusted to haggle.

He had determined, after the Scopes trial, to taper off his practice. The trial of a criminal case can be cruelly exhausting —physically, mentally, and emotionally—and Darrow felt that he had had too many of them. A social and political history of the twentieth century could not be written without including many of his landmark cases. He had represented Eugene Debs in a political prosecution arising out of the Pullman strike and labor violence of 1894. He had gained an acquittal on a murder charge against Big Bill Heywood in Idaho in 1905 in labor warfare between the Western Federation of Miners and labor-busting mine owners. He had represented the American Federation of Labor in saving the McNamara brothers from the gallows in 1910, following the twenty-one deaths caused by the bombing of the Los Angeles Times Building in 1910.

He had from that time on become the most sought-after criminal lawyer in the country and by 1925 had appeared in over fifty murder cases. In between trials he lectured and debated constantly against capital punishment and, following the adoption of the Eighteenth Amendment, against Prohibition, which he considered a spectacular piece of folly.

But what particularly attracted Du Bois and the NAACP to Darrow, aside from his skill as a lawyer, was his interest in race relations and a speech about John Brown that Darrow would deliver, from time to time, on the lecture circuit. One of Darrow's biographers writes of John Brown visiting Darrow's father in Kinsman, Ohio, and saying to five-year-old Clarence, "The Negro has too few friends; and you and I must never desert him."

This makes a nice story, but it cannot be true. John Brown died on the gallows in 1859 when Clarence Darrow was only two years old. Darrow, of course, does not mention any such incident in his autobiography, nor does he tell of any meeting between his father and Brown. But there is no doubt that John Brown was one of Darrow's favorite characters. He was fascinated by the Old Testament prophetic vision, by the fanaticism, and especially by the radicalism. Audiences hearing Darrow's John Brown lecture came away convinced that Clarence Darrow felt that what the world needed was more raids against more Harpers Ferries and that Darrow would like to lead them.

John Brown was born in Connecticut in 1800. His parents were farmers and like all who really work were poor. His natural instincts were never warped or smoothed or numbed by learning. His mind was so strong, his sense of justice so keen, and his sympathies so deep, that he might have been able to even withstand an education. He believed in destiny and in God. He was narrow, fanatical, and self-willed; like all men who deeply impress the generation in which they live. Had he been broad and profound, he would have asked himself the question, "What is the use?" and the answer would have brought an easy life and a peaceful death. He was a man of one idea, which is all that the brain of any man of action can ever hold. . . .

He was of the type of Cromwell, of Calvin, of Mahomet; not a good type for the peace of the world, but a type that here and there down through the ages has been needful to kindle a flame that should burn the decaying institutions and ancient wrongs in the crucible of a world's awakening wrath. . . .

John Brown found the power of slavery thoroughly entrenched in the United States. No other institution in the land seemed more secure. True, here and there, voices were raised to denounce the curse, but for the most part these came only from the weak, the poor and the despised. The pulpit, the press, the courts, the wealthy and respectable gave it their sanction; and more powerful still was the fact that slavery was hopelessly interwoven with the commercial and financial institutions of the land and any attack on this was an attack on the sacred rights of property—the sin of sins!

When the slave power, reaching out its arm to perpetuate itself, turned to Kansas to fasten its shackles on a new state, John Brown sent forth four devoted sons and two others of his kinsmen to help fight the battle of freedom in this new land.

It is idle to ask or answer the question as to where the blame should be placed for any special act through these bloody days and nights. The war was not between men, but between two systems, old as the human race; freedom and slavery. Then, as ever, officials and power and wealth were with slavery and the dreamer and the idealist with liberty. Then, as ever, the power of slavery was united, and the forces of freedom divided. Fighting for liberty were the Garrisons, who believed in non-resistance; the Beechers, who believed in appealing to the heart, the heart of a system that had no heart; the Sewards and Sumners who believed in the ballot; and John Brown who believed all this meant war and could be settled by no other method save that of war. . . .

Guerrilla warfare was the order of the day. Guerrilla warfare was murder because the killed are so very few. In this warfare, the name of Brown was a terror to the other side. He was silent, active, resolute and unyielding; next to his belief in abolition he believed in God. None of his band drank, smoked, told doubtful stories, jested on sacred things, or indulged in levity of any kind. They had daily prayers, stern visages, frequent Bible readings, and they knew how to shoot. . . .

Darrow would then describe how John Brown, his four sons, five other whites, and seven blacks raided Harpers Ferry and captured the arsenal which they hoped would arm a guerrilla army in the nearby mountains for an all-out attack on slavery. Brown and his band were, of course, quickly captured, some shot, and the others hanged.

Darrow left no doubt that in his view Brown's work had been useful, necessary, and, eventually, successful.

The news of John Brown's raid sent an electric shock around the world; the slave power was aghast at the audacity of the act, and knew not where to turn. The leading abolitionists of the North were stunned and terrified at the manhunt coming on. The great William Lloyd Garrison promptly and fiercely denounced Brown's mad act. Beecher and Seward cried out against the man who had so criminally and recklessly hazarded his friends and the cause. Bold and wrathful were all these old abolitionists when there was no risk to run, but here was a maniac who transformed their words to deeds; with grand juries and inquisitions abroad in the land, no one's neck was safe.

In the first mad days but one man stood fearless and unmoved while the universe was falling around his head, and this was John Brown. When faint voices cried out for his rescue, Brown promptly made reply: "I do not know but that I ought to discourage any attempt to save my life. I think I cannot now better serve the cause I love than to die for it, and in my death I may do more than in my life."

But soon the mad frenzy of the mob began to die away. A few brave souls stood unmoved in the fury of the storm. While Brown still lived, the calm, sane voice of Ralph Waldo Emerson called his countrymen to view Brown's deeds in the light of the motives that fired his soul; he told the world that soon the day would come when his deeds with their motives would place John Brown among the martyrs and heroes of the earth. . . .

But while the victorious hosts were destroying the infamous system that had cursed the earth so long, John Brown was sleeping in a felon's grave and around his decaying neck was the black mark of the hangman's noose, the reward of a Christian world for the devoted soul that had made the supreme sacrifice for his loyalty and love. More than any other man, his mad raid broke the bondman's chain. . . .

The world has long since accepted the results of John

Brown's work. Great as was the cost all men know that it was worth the price. But even now the idle, carping and foolish still ask, "Did John Brown do right and would it not better have been done some other way?" Of all the foolish questions asked by idle tongues the most childish is to ask if a great work should not have been done some other way. . . .

The radicals of today are the conservatives of tomorrow. . . . The earth needs and will always need John Browns. . . .

There was not a chance that the man who wrote these words would refuse to represent Ossian Sweet, who had had his own Harpers Ferry in Detroit. Yet, when the NAACP committee called on him at Hays' home in early October, he tried to beg off. But even as he gave excuses, he knew he would go to Detroit. Darrow was not modest about his own abilities and he had said, "Defending Negroes, even in the North, was no boy's job, although boys usually were given that responsibility." He was determined that Sweet would be defended by men and he agreed to leave at once for Detroit with Hays, who had already agreed to enter the case.

VIII

A Jury of Their Peers

Ten colored men and one woman are in this indictment, tried by twelve jurors, gentlemen. Every one of you are white, aren't you? At least you all think so. We haven't one colored man in the jury. We couldn't get one. One was called and he was disqualified. You twelve white men are trying a colored man on race prejudice. Now, let me ask you whether you are not prejudiced. I want to put this square to you, gentlemen. I haven't any doubt but that everyone of you are prejudiced against colored people. I want you to guard against it. I want you to do all you can to be fair in this case and I believe you will. . . . You have seen some of the colored people in this case. They have been so far above the white people that live at the corner of Garland and Charlevoix that they can't be compared intellectually, morally and physically, and you know it.

Darrow was dismayed, but not surprised, by the strong feeling in Detroit against the defendants. As he was later to write, "Few colored men in America charged with killing white persons have ever lived to tell the tale; they have been lucky if they survived long enough to be tried in court under the forms of law and legally slaughtered."

Being legally slaughtered was at least one thing the defendants did not have to fear. Michigan had abolished capital punishment in 1846 but Darrow had no doubt, after conferring with the prosecutor and reading the records and newspaper accounts of the case, that public sentiment would demand a vigorous prosecution and the maximum punishment—imprisonment for life—for all eleven defendants. That punishment seemed ridiculously disproportionate to the alleged crime and Darrow felt that another community, not quite so panic-stricken over the prospect of blacks living next door to whites, might offer a more reasonable atmosphere for the trial. Detroit, in October, 1925, was probably the worst place in the country for such a trial, from the defendants' standpoint. In addition to the tensions created by the killing of Leon Breiner and the other black-white confrontations of the summer, the city was being lacerated daily with charges and countercharges in the mayoral race from the supporters of Mayor Smith, the Catholic, and Charles Bowles, the Ku Klux Klan candidate. The trial was scheduled to commence on October 30, only one week before the election, when feelings were certain to be high. The campaign had already produced wildly irrational effects and Darrow wanted nothing more than reason to prevail.

But reason had fled Detroit. The Klan candidate was even attracting substantial support among Detroit's Jewish population, solely because Henry Ford was supporting Mayor Smith. Ford had sorely offended Jews throughout the country by publishing in his Dearborn newspaper the spurious and slanderous *Protocols of Zion,* and in 1925 any friend of Ford's was automatically suspect among Jews.

The first decision Darrow had to make, then, was whether or not to seek a change of venue. Some degree of white hostility to blacks would almost certainly be encountered in any community to which the case might be moved, but in another city the trial atmosphere would not be further polluted by the bitterness of an election campaign revolving, at least in part, around the issue of race.

But Darrow had been greatly impressed, at a pretrial conference before Judge Murphy, with Murphy's intelligence and with what Darrow sensed was a great capacity for fairness and compassion. Darrow had spent his life appraising judges and jurors and it was his experience that though jurors were very much alike from state to state and city to city, judges were very different indeed, and he decided to risk the potential disadvantage of trial in Detroit for the potential benefit of a decent and honorable judge. He did not ask for a change of venue.

He did renew the motion for bail for the ten defendants who were still in jail, this time making the additional argument that preparation of the defense would be prejudiced if the defendants were not accessible at all times for consultation with their lawyers. However, Judge Murphy's compassion was not yet awakened and the defendants remained in jail. Darrow hated jails and he left most of the pretrial interviews to Hays and the Detroit lawyers while he devoted his time to preparation for the questioning and selection of jurors—a function that he considered the most important part of any criminal case and most especially a case in which the most important witnesses would be bigotry and racial fear.

Anglo-Saxon law has borrowed from the French a procedural device known as *voir dire,* which consists of a brief examination of a prospective witness or juror to the end that the judge might make a judgment as to whether or not he has any interest or bias in the cause that would make it impossible for him to speak the truth. We have retained the name but greatly expanded the procedure. The questioning is now done, at least in state court criminal proceedings, not by the judge but by the lawyers, and often more time is consumed in selecting jurors than in presenting evidence. For most lawyers it is wasted time since every prospective juror is convinced that he is an outstandingly honest fellow incapable of prejudice, unfairness, or arbitrariness, and a juror will rarely respond to a question in such a manner as to indicate that he will not speak the truth. Most challenges to jurors, therefore, are arbitrary and meaningless at least insofar as they are based on jurors' answers to questions. Darrow was not interested at all in the answers that his questions elicited. He was interested only in the questions and in using those questions to educate the jury, to create an atmosphere, to force the jury to examine its own attitudes and to ask itself questions.

Darrow's challenges to prospective jurors were not based on his questions but on his own set of standards, which did not vary from case to case and which were formed out of his own experience. The standards were far from scientific and his challenges could have been made without any questions—simply by examining the faces of the panel and the biographical data with which each lawyer was furnished. His system was part intuition and part superstition, part sociology and part psychology, part logic and part guesswork. He would almost always challenge a German or a Swede and almost always accept an Irishman or a Jew. He chose younger jurors over older and working people over professional people.

Darrow himself had always claimed that no lawyer really wants a juror who is fair:

> The state wants a juror who has grown old, serious, unimaginative, and a Presbyterian, if possible. The lawyers for the defense want a man who is alert, witty, emotional, and who is a Catholic, or without any religious faith whatsoever. No one ever judges anyone else without finding him guilty, no one ever understands another without being in sympathy with him. A person who can understand can comprehend why, and that leaves no field for condemning.

And so, Clarence Darrow set out to teach the jurors understanding. The jury panel numbered 150 when court convened on October 30. It proved to be not enough. Under Michigan law the defense was permitted 30 peremptory challenges for each defendant, which meant that Darrow, if he chose, could, for any reason, or for no reason, excuse 330 prospective jurors. The state had only 15 peremptory challenges for each defendant, or a total of 155, but it really needed only one—that to excuse the lone black included in the original panel of 150 and the additional panel of 50 which had to be called before a jury could be impaneled. The presence of only one black man out of 200 veniremen called for prospective jury duty might today create a presumption of a systematic exclusion of blacks from the jury and give rise to a constitutional question. But the innocence and arrogance of 1925 did not doubt that justice could be rendered to blacks by whites. (It is still dangerous to be skeptical of this article of faith. In April, 1970, Kingman Brewster, president of Yale University, was severely criticized in most quarters for expressing doubt that a black revolutionary could receive a fair trial anywhere in the United States.)

In addition to peremptory challenges, each side had the right to an unlimited number of challenges for cause if upon *voir dire* it appeared that there was bias or interest in the cause, or acquaintanceship with parties or counsel, so as to preclude, in the opinion of the court, an impartial weighing of the facts by the juror challenged.

A strict application of this principle would have made it virtually impossible to select a jury among the white people of Detroit in 1925. Almost every venireman, while asserting that he believed that blacks should have the right to live wherever they desired, also stated under further questioning that the right should be waived by a black if it appeared that he was not welcome in the neighborhood. Any twelve jurors picked at random would probably have been as good as any other because this was the attitude of white America in 1925, if not in 1971. Accordingly, Darrow wasted little time in trying to show individual bias or partiality and used the time instead in interweaving into his examination a short history of the black man in America and in asking questions calculated to provoke some self-examination by the jurors. Do you know any blacks? Would you call them friends? Have you ever visited their homes? Have they visited yours? Why not? Do you consider them different from you? In what respect? Why is it that you cannot recall the last name of the lady you say has worked in your kitchen for two years? Does she have a family? Does she have a home? Does she have a life?

Darrow actually challenged fewer prospective jurors than was his usual practice. Only those who he judged would be clearly hostile were dismissed. Those about whom he had only some doubt he passed. In that crowd there would always be some doubt and there was always danger that the next man would be worse. Only one man on the panel admitted to being a member of the Ku Klux Klan and he was, of course, dismissed, even though he claimed that he was not prejudiced against blacks, only foreigners. Darrow was never certain that one or two other members of the jury he finally accepted were not secret members of the Klan, though he had tried to reduce that possibility by retaining as many jurors as possible with foreign-sounding names and by avoiding those with southern backgrounds. He also managed to keep four Catholics on the jury (though questions concerning religion were not permitted, Darrow had had an independent investigation made of the background of the entire panel). So far as he knew he had no Presbyterians.

After one week of *voir dire* Darrow felt that he had gone as far as he could in trying to educate the jury and to awaken some compassion and understanding. He had no illusions that he had stamped out bigotry, prejudice, and ignorance and that the twelve good men and true left in the jury box were in any sense an impartial jury. Their partiality to white skin made that impossible. But then he had never had, and had never hoped for, an impartial jury. His own evaluation was:

> We managed to get twelve men who said they could
> be fair, but of course they knew nothing about that.
> No one knows so little about a man's ability to be fair
> as the man himself. To a man himself all his opinions,

attitudes and prejudices are fair or he would not hold
them.

All that he had hoped to do was to make this jury aware of,
and perhaps to question, some of those attitudes, opinions,
and prejudices so that they could recognize them when they
were expressed from the witness stand. What he hoped to
show was that, regardless of who fired the fatal shot, what
really killed Leon Breiner was attitudes, opinions, and prejudices.

IX

The Conspiracy

Mr. Moll took particular pains to say to you, gentlemen,
that these eleven people here are guilty of murder; he
calls this a cold-blooded, deliberate and premeditated
murder; that is, they were there to kill. That was their
purpose. Eleven, he said—amongst that eleven is Mrs.
Sweet. The wife of Dr. Sweet, she is a murderer, gentlemen? The State's attorney said so, and the assistant
State's attorney said so. . . . Pray, tell me what has
Mrs. Sweet done to make her a murderer? She is the wife
of Dr. Sweet. She is the mother of a little baby. She left
the child at her mother's home while she moved into this
highly cultured community near Goethe Street. Anyhow,
the baby was to be safe; but she took her own chance,
and she didn't have a gun; none was provided for her.
Brother Toms drew from the witnesses that there were
ten guns, and ten men. He didn't leave any for her. Maybe
she had a penknife, but there is no evidence on that question. What did she do, gentlemen? She is put down here
as a murderer. She wasn't even upstairs. She didn't even
look out of a window. She was down in the back kitchen
cooking a ham to feed her family and friends, and a white
mob came to drive them out of their home before the
ham was served for dinner. She is a murderer, and all of
these defendants who were driven out of their home
must go to the penitentiary for life if you can find twelve

jurors somewhere who have enough prejudice in their hearts and hatred in their minds. Now, that is this case, gentlemen, and that is all there is to this case. Take the hatred away and you have nothing left.

The Wayne County prosecutor in 1925 was Robert M. Toms, a man who believed in a well-rounded staff. He had appointed a black as one of his assistant prosecutors but for balance he had appointed two whites who were reputed to be Klan members. Toms himself had been charged with being a Klansman when he had run for reelection in 1924, a charge which he denied. Toms liked to say that he was a prosecutor and not a persecutor and once was quoted as saying, "Many prosecutors feel they must be hard-boiled gents, bent on filling the Bastille with permanent customers or giving the hangman plenty of business. I'd rather see a prosecutor who made a record of keeping cases out of court which had no business there."

Adherence to that policy was not apparent in Toms' vigorous prosecution of the Sweet case. He assigned his most aggressive and most ambitious assistant, Lester S. Moll, to assist him in the prosecution. Nothing could boost a political career faster in 1925 than sending blacks to jail in a racially inflamed city and both Toms and Moll, beginning with their strenuous opposition to the granting of bail down to the final word of their final argument, were indeed bent on making the eleven defendants permanent residents of the Bastille. In any event there would be no business for the hangman.

The prosecution realized, of course, that it would not be possible to prove which defendant fired the shot that killed Leon Breiner. This in no way added to the difficulty of their case since they were able to call on the prosecutor's delight— a conspiracy theory. Then, as now, prosecutors faced with problems of proof of individual responsibility cured the infirmity by using the conspiracy crutch. The State claimed that all the defendants illegally agreed and conspired to arm themselves, with premeditated and malicious intent to shoot to kill, without provocation and without justification. Pursuant to that conspiracy, the State argued, one of the defendants, and it mattered not which one, fired the shot that killed Leon Breiner. Therefore, all were guilty of first-degree murder.

This kind of bootstrap justice is becoming more and more irresistible to American law enforcement agencies. If demonstrations lead to violence, either because of overenthusiasm of the demonstrators, or overzealousness of the law enforcers, or both, then simply claim that the demonstrators have conspired to commit violence. If troubled opponents of war exercise their right of free speech to criticize war and draft laws, and individually they have committed no crime, then simply charge them with conspiracy to encourage and abet draft evasion.

The law of conspiracy has been called the evil genius of the common law. Nothing like it existed in Roman law nor did it have a counterpart in any of the European legal codes. It seems to have first appeared in sixteenth-century England as a civil action against a combination to procure a false indictment and was soon expanded to include any combination to defeat the administration of law. The concept was broadened to encompass any joint action to commit immoral or criminal acts, thus opening the door to the suppression of virtually any activity which the prevailing morality considered threatening. Almost immediately the law of conspiracy began to be used to imprison workers who joined together in demands for higher wages or better working conditions. Thus, in 1721, in *Rex* v. *The Journeymen Tailors,* an English court held that one tailor alone may demand higher wages, but if he joins with fellow tailors to do so, it is a criminal conspiracy against his employer and the king. This really seems to have been an ad hoc ruling which the court considered necessary in order to protect employers, because the authority cited as precedent —*The Tubwomen* v. *The Brewers of London*—apparently did not exist. At least no report of such a case has ever been found nor is there any reference to it prior to the *Tailors* case. The law of conspiracy is, to a large degree, a historical accident and rests on the shaky precedent of cases hardly more authentic than the probably apocryphal *Tubwomen* of London.

Though the original concept of conspiracy had seemed to be limited to a combination to effect a criminal act by noncriminal means, or a noncriminal act by criminal means, the criminality ingredient had been replaced by mere unlawfulness and unlawful came to mean, in conspiracy law, simply wrongful according to the judge's own notion of undesirable conduct. American courts found the device as useful as the English in repressing activities deemed to be antisocial. A New Hampshire court in 1844 in a criminal conspiracy case held that criminal conduct, in the traditional sense, was not required:

> It will be enough if they are corrupt, dishonest, fraudulent or immoral, and in that sense illegal, and it is in the combination to make use of such practices, that the dangers of this offense consist.
>
> (*State v. Birnham,* 1844)

American courts throughout the nineteenth century had no difficulty in finding the joint efforts of laborers against employers to be "corrupt, dishonest, fraudulent or immoral" and workingmen seeking nothing more than higher wages suddenly found themselves branded as criminals.

Thus, a Pennsylvania court held:

> A combination of workmen to raise their wages may be considered in a twofold point of view: one is to benefit themselves . . . the other is to injure those who do not join their society. The rule of law condemns both.
>
> (*Philadelphia Cordewainers case,* 1806)

The rule of law, however, did not condemn conspiring employers because a later Pennsylvania case in which journeymen shoemakers sought to have employers indicted for combining to depress wages called this simply "a combination to resist oppression . . . and therefore, perfectly innocent." (*Common-wealth* v. *Carlisle*, 1821)

When workingmen finally acquired enough political power to resist this kind of repression, the conspiracy attack shifted from economic grounds to political and social grounds and the country's law courts have been busy in recent decades in prosecuting the real or fancied dangers in conspiracies to overthrow the government, to evade the draft, to incite riot, and, in far too many cases, to punish what is considered to be antisocial action in cases where individual responsibility, which we like to tell ourselves is the bedrock of our society, cannot be established.

Such a case was the Sweet trial where the Sweets, by defiantly moving into their house with the intention of defending it thereby, according to the prevailing morality, were being "corrupt, dishonest, fraudulent or immoral" in combination, and since someone was killed, this was a conspiracy to commit murder.

Conspiracies abounded in Detroit in 1925. The Sweets and their friends no doubt conspired to defend their home and their persons against injury and violence. The waterworks improvers conspired to drive them from that home. But the worst conspiracy of all, and the real insult to democracy, was the conspiracy of the police and prosecution to portray the killing of Leon Breiner as a premeditated, malicious act of murder unprovoked by any aggression or hostility of the crowd—indeed to even argue, until such arguments became absurd, that no crowd existed on the corner of Garland and Charlevoix on September 9.

Years later, in 1941, prosecutor Toms (then Judge Toms along with his colleague Judge Moll) was to say, "There were probably more people around the Sweet house than the people's witnesses testified. At any rate there were enough to frighten a group of nervous, apprehensive Negroes who anticipated trouble."

If Toms knew this in 1941, then he certainly knew or should have known it in 1925. Yet he permitted Moll, in his opening statement, to paint a picture of a friendly, peaceful neighborhood whose peace and calm were shattered by gunfire from the hostile element which had invaded it. Of course, Moll told the jury, Negroes have the right to live wherever they choose; Negroes have all the rights that whites have. But we all have rights which we, as good citizens, yield and surrender to the greater good of peace and harmony and the preservation of an orderly society. The important thing, Toms said, is to conform to the standards of the community—even if that means giving up rights. Toms illustrated this proposition with some bizarre examples. One has a right to grab a seat in a streetcar before a woman gets to it. One has a right to attend a dance in a bathing suit. One has the right to put his feet on the table or take off his shoes in the parlor. But these things are not done, Moll said, because they don't conform to practice.

It is difficult to believe that Moll could seriously equate the right to defend one's self, one's home, one's dignity, and one's manhood with this absurd list of Emily Post rules; but Arthur Garfield Hays, who preserved that portion of Moll's statement for posterity, had no doubt that Moll, a deadly serious man, really believed the nonsense. Darrow considered it too silly for his attention and diligently, if perhaps ostentatiously, worked on a crossword puzzle while Moll talked.

Moll ended his opening statement by telling the jury that this was not a case of self-defense; not a case of racial prejudice; not a case of accidental death occurring in the midst of chaos and confusion; but simply a case of cold-blooded murder committed with malice aforethought. He then proceeded to call the first of his seventy witnesses, almost all of whom would testify that each was at the corner of Garland and Charlevoix on the evening of September 9, and that there was no crowd there. Apparently none of these witnesses saw the other sixty-nine, not to mention the several hundreds who, at one time or another, were in the immediate vicinity on that unhappy night.

X

How to Maintain
Property Values

Now, perhaps some of you gentlemen do not believe in colored men moving into white neighborhoods. Let me talk about that a minute, gentlemen. I don't want to leave any question untouched that might be important in this case, and I fancy that some of you do not believe as I believe on this question. Let us be honest about it. There are people who buy themselves a little home and think the value of it would go down if colored people come. Perhaps it would. I don't know. I am not going to testify in this case. It may go down and it may go up. It will probably go down for some purposes and up for others. I don't know. Suppose it does. What of it? I am sorry for anybody whose home depreciates in value. Still you cannot keep up a government for the purpose of making people's homes valuable. Noise will depreciate the value of a house, and sometimes a streetcar line will do it. A public school will do it. People do not like a lot of children around their house. That is one reason why they send them to school.—Livery stables used to do it: garages do it now.—No man can buy a house and be sure that somebody will not depreciate its value. Something may enhance its value, of course. We are always willing to take the profit but not willing to take the loss. Those are incidents of civilization. We get that because we refuse to live with our fellow man, that is all. . . . Do I need to say anything about it? You, gentlemen, are here and you want to do right. Are you going to invite colored people to live next door to you? No. Would it hurt you? Not at all.

Before the first witness had finished his testimony there was trouble inside and outside the courtroom. Upon returning from the morning recess, one of the jurors reported to Judge Murphy that a black lady in the corridor had threatened the jury as they filed past, warning that the blacks of Detroit were watching them. The alleged culprit denied making such a threat but the judge warned her not to do it again in any event.

The incident gave Darrow an opportunity to complain to Judge Murphy that the reason there were so many blacks in the hallways was because the courtroom attendants were apparently reserving most of the spectators' seats for whites. He had noticed a conspicuous absence of black faces during the *voir dire* and had asked the bailiff why most of those inside appeared to be white, while outside the color was mostly black. He had been assured that attendance was on a first-come-first-served basis but the faces in the gallery remained mostly white. Judge Murphy then ordered that half the spectators' section be reserved for blacks. For the first few days blacks and whites intermingled in the crowd but gradually, as though some natural process of segregation were taking place, the colors began to separate until the gallery was divided into all-black and all-white areas, like neighborhoods in Detroit and the country in general.

On the afternoon of the first day of testimony, the trial almost came to an abrupt end. During the testimony of the coroner, who was describing the wound that killed Leon Breiner, a woman seated in the first row of the spectators' section fainted. Judge Murphy immediately declared a recess and ordered the jury to retire to the jury room. The woman, as the judge, the prosecution, and the defense all knew, was Mrs. Leon Breiner. The question was whether or not the jury also knew who she was and how they would be affected by the incident.

Darrow, out of the presence of the jury, suggested to the court that Mrs. Breiner had not really fainted but that she and the prosecution had staged the performance for whatever psychological benefit the prosecution might derive from it. Darrow may or may not have believed this, but it gave him an opportunity to put the prosecutor on the defense—something he sought to do in each of his trials. Darrow decided against moving for a mistrial when the jury, under questioning by the judge, claimed not to know the identity of the woman who fainted, and Darrow could see no indication that the episode had had any effect whatsoever.

As the prosecution began its long parade of witnesses to the stand, Darrow put away his crossword puzzles. The first were medical witnesses and Darrow immediately elicited valuable testimony from them on cross-examination. They conceded that since no bullet was found in Leon Breiner's body, nor any bullet near the body which could be connected with the wound, it was not possible to establish, with any degree of certainty, the kind of gun which had fired the shot.

The corner had described the wound as a "round penetrating wound at the level of the last lumbar and one inch to the left of same, passing through the abdomen and making exit three inches below and two inches to the left of the umbilicus or the belly button."

In other words, Breiner had been shot in the back, a revelation that the prosecution thought would outrage the sense of fair play of the jury, which, by 1925, had already seen enough Western movies to know that it is decidedly un-American to shoot someone in the back. But the coroner's testimony was more or less neutralized when he admitted that, based on the nature of the wound, the shot could just as well have been fired from the ground level—say the sidewalk—as from the higher elevation of the Sweet house across the street.

The coroner was the last witness before adjournment. The first day's testimony had been productive but not spectacular. The following morning's *Free Press* reported:

> So far Darrow's pleading has not set the Detroit River on fire, but there is evidence of the latent force of his personality. Though he is homely in manner, dress and speech, there is a tenacity and vigor in his questions which bespeak a bulldog grip of the testimony at every stage of its development and an appreciation of the potentialities which arise as the case is being unfolded.
>
> The galluses which featured his appearance at Dayton are not in view, but their place is taken by the armholes of his vest, the place of repose of his thumbs when things are proceeding more or less normally. When he wishes to press a witness his left arm hangs limp by his gangling figure, while his right is thrust directly out from the shoulder, his index finger moving convulsively as he punctuates his questions.

The next two days were devoted solely to police testimony. Darrow had studied the transcript of the preliminary hearing and his purposes would be perfectly served if the police merely repeated what they had said then. The defense investigation had turned up enough independent witnesses who were likely to be credible to the jury so that the police account of the number of people at the scene of the activity just prior to the shooting would be shown to be patently false.

But Toms and Moll had realized that the police testimony at the preliminary hearing had created a credibility gap and all the police witnesses at the trial revised their crowd estimates upwards. Inspector Schuknecht gave some testimony that he had not given at the earlier hearing, presumably in the hope of clarifying what appeared to have been a somewhat ambiguous role played by the police: "I informed the men before we left the station that Dr. Sweet would be permitted to occupy his house, even if it took every man in the department to protect him." Schuknecht, on cross-examination, professed to see no difference between this statement and his earlier testimony when he had said that his instructions to his men were simply to "protect life and property," without saying whose life or which property.

The prosecution was also aware that the case against Mrs. Sweet was the most tenuous of all, and so the police account of finding the guns and ammunition was expanded to include a description of a small black traveling bag found in the house with a label reading Madame O. H. Sweet, Paris, and containing "several varieties of ammunition, shells, and cartridges."

The police steadfastly and unanimously testified that the defendants had not been denied the right to see lawyers before making their statements. They simply had not asked for lawyers, so how could the police have denied them the right? The record was clear, however, that Charles Mahoney, one of the Detroit counsel, had been forced to file a writ of *habeas corpus* before any lawyer was permitted to see the defendants.

The officer who supervised the interrogation made it quite clear that counsel would have been denied even if requested. Lieutenant William Johnson denied knowing that Mahoney had appeared at the station and had not been permitted to see the defendants. Darrow asked:

> "Do you know Mr. Mahoney?"
> "Yes."
> "Would you have admitted him had he come?"
> "I hardly think I would."

Clearly, to Lieutenant Johnson, it was an outrageous suggestion that suspects have access to lawyers until the police are ready for them to have lawyers.

Darrow continued:

> "Did you ever get a statement from a prisoner except voluntarily?"
> "No."

"Did you say to Mahoney at the police station 'get the hell out of here'?"

"No."

"What were you in the room for when the statements were being made?"

"To check up on them."

Asked what the purpose of taking the statements was, Johnson said, "For the purpose of giving the prisoner a square deal."

To the same purpose, no doubt, the police and prosecutors had carefully coached each of the civilian witnesses to minimize the number of people in the vicinity of Garland and Charlevoix on the night of the shooting.

But they were not so accustomed to a courtroom as the police and every now and then a witness would slip a little on cross-examination. Florence Ware, who lived two blocks away, admitted she had gone to the corner of Garland and Charlevoix out of curiosity.

"Curiosity as to what?"

"The crowd," she began and then hastily struck the forbidden word and insisted that no crowd had been there.

One witness, a boy of sixteen, forgot his lines completely.

Witness: There was a great crowd—no, I won't say a great crowd, a large crowd—well there were a few people there and the officers were keeping them moving.

Darrow: Have you talked to anyone about this case?

Witness: Lieutenant Johnson.

Darrow: And when you started to answer the question you forgot to say "a few people" didn't you?

Witness: Yes sir.

For the most part witness after witness responded to questions about the size of the crowd as though by rote:

"What were you doing there?"

"I live nearby."

"What brought you to that corner?"

"Curiosity."

"About what?"

"Nothing in particular."

"You know that colored people had moved into that house."

"Yes."

"Did that have anything to do with your curiosity?"

"Maybe."

"Many people there?"

"No."

"Were there strangers there—people that you didn't ordinarily see in the neighborhood?"

"Some."

"How many?"

"Twenty-five or thirty."

What concerned Darrow much more than the lies about the size and nature of the mob so artlessly told by the witnesses was their pride in being members of the Waterworks Improvement Association and their shameless belief in the association's shameful goal of keeping the neighborhood color-clean. These hard-working God-fearing people did not doubt for a moment the necessity to maintain their property values by excluding blacks.

The sanctity of private property was, after all, what America was all about, and no less an institution than the United States Supreme Court had affirmed and reaffirmed that separation of the races was legal, right, and proper.

The witnesses' answers to Darrow on this subject were much more freely given. Thus, when Darrow questioned Eben Draper:

Q: Did that [Sweet buying the house] have anything to do with your joining the club?

A: Possibly.

Q: Did it?

A: Yes.

Q: You joined the club to aid in keeping that a white district?

A: Yes.

Q: At the meeting in the school was any reference made to keeping the district free from colored people?

A: Yes.

Q: How many people were present at that meeting?

A: Seven hundred.

Another witness, John Minot, was just as direct.

Q: Did you join the organization as a property owner?

A: I did.

Q: What was your object?

A: To keep the neighborhood up to its existing high standard.

Q: Your interest was in keeping Negroes out to maintain the value of your property?

A: Yes.

Alfred Andrews told about the pep talk by the man from the Tireman Improvement Association:

Q: Did he tell you about any race riot trouble they had in his neighborhood?

A: Yes, he told us about a Negro named Dr. Turner who had bought a house on Spokane Avenue.

Q: Did he say his organization made Turner leave?

A: Yes. He said his organization wouldn't have Negroes in their neighborhood and that they would cooperate with us in keeping them out of ours.

Q: Did the crowd applaud him?

A: Yes.

Q: Did you applaud?

A: Yes.

Q: You feel that way now?

A: Yes, I haven't changed.

Q: You know a colored man has certain rights?

A: Yes, I was in favor of keeping the Sweets out by legal means.

Q: Did the speaker talk of legal means?

A: No, he was a radical. I myself do not believe in violence.

Q: Did anybody in that audience of five hundred or more people protest against the speaker's advocacy of violence?

A: I don't know.

Ray Dove, who lived directly across the street from the Sweet home, was another believer in the racial purity of the neighborhood.

Q: You didn't want him there?

A: I am not prejudiced against them, but I don't believe in mixing whites and blacks.

Q: So you didn't want him there?

A: No, I guess not.

Dove claimed not to have known that for two years he had had a black for a neighbor. This remarkable lack of perception was shared by John Gratke who lived right next door to the Sweet house and who claimed not to have known that Mrs. Smith's husband was black:

Q: Now do you know who was there before the family came there—just before the Sweets came in?

A: I understand a Mrs. Smith owned the house.

Q: Now, Mrs. Smith's husband was named Ed Smith, wasn't he?

A: I don't know.

Q: Did you ever see her husband?

A: I don't say as I did.

Q: How long did Mrs. Smith live there?

A: I should say about two years.

Q: And in two years you never saw a man there?

A: I don't say I never saw a man there.
Q: Well, the Smith that lived there?
A: I never met Mr. Smith.
Q: You knew Mr. Smith was a colored man, didn't you?
A: No, sir, I didn't.
Q: Never saw him there?
A: No, sir.
Q: Never saw a tall colored man in the house?
A: No, sir.

But Gratke was a much more observant witness of the events of September 9. He claimed to have been sitting on the porch when shots were fired from the Sweet house for no apparent reason. His membership in the Waterworks Improvement Association had nothing to do with the Sweets, he said, though he did not approve of their moving into the neighborhood.

Darrow had no doubt that under similar circumstances most of the all-white jury would have joined an improvement association dedicated to maintaining "property values" by keeping a neighborhood white. He had no reason to hope that this jury subscribed to the prevailing mythology any less than the rest of white America. It would be difficult, therefore, for the jury to consider anything the neighbors did in pursuit of their noble goal as sufficient justification for the measures that the Sweets took in response, and the plea of self-defense, of course, depended on the jury finding that the force used by the Sweets was reasonable under the circumstances. As always, the white man would measure a black man's actions by the white man's standards. Whites, who could live anywhere, believed that no white man would live where he was not wanted and it was therefore unreasonable for any black man to live where he was not wanted. Any action a black man took in defense of such an unreasonable goal could hardly be reasonable.

XI

A Black Studies Program

My friend, Moll, said that my client here was a coward.
A coward, gentlemen. Here, he says, were a gang of gunmen, and cowards—shot Breiner through the back. Nobody
saw Breiner, of course. If he had his face turned toward
the house, while he was smoking there, waiting for the
shooting to begin, it wasn't our fault. . . . If he had been
at home, it would not have happened. Who are the
cowards in this case? Cowards, gentlemen! Eleven people
with black skins, eleven people, gentlemen, whose ancestors did not come to America because they wanted to,
but were brought here in slave ships, to toil for nothing,
for the whites—whose lives have been taken in nearly
every state in the Union,—they have been victims of riots
all over this land of the free. They have had to take
what is left after everybody else has grabbed what he
wanted. The only place where he has been put in front
is on the battle field. When we are fighting we give him
a chance to die, and the best chance. But, everywhere
else he has been food for the flames and the ropes, and
the knives and the guns and hate of the white, regardless
of law and liberty, and the common sentiments of justice
that should move men. Were they cowards? No, gentlemen, they may have been gunmen. They may have tried

to murder, but they were not cowards. Eleven people knowing what it meant, with the history of the race behind them, with the picture of Detroit in front of them—with the knowledge of shootings and killings and insult and injury without end, eleven of them go into a house, gentlemen, with no police protection, in the face of a mob, and the hatred of a community, and take guns and ammunition and fight for their rights, and for your rights and mine, and for the rights of every being that lives. They went in and faced a mob seeking to tear them to bits. Call them something beside cowards. The cowardly curs were in the mob gathered there with the backing of the law.

As the dreary procession of witnesses succeeded each other on the stand, Darrow began to have second thoughts about his decision to entrust the fate of his clients to a jury rather than to Judge Murphy on a jury waiver. So deeply ingrained were these white attitudes of racial superiority, that Darrow began to fear that a jury, regardless of the evidence, would find black defendants guilty of the crime charged because, in their eyes, these blacks had caused the trouble that ensued by daring to move into the neighborhood and then, to compound the crime, by insisting on their right to remain. The jury might feel compelled to express their displeasure at such nonservile behavior. A guilty verdict would show these defendants and the rest of black America that it is dangerous to forget one's place in white America.

Accordingly, after the last of the State's seventy witnesses had finished his testimony, Darrow and Hays were ready with their motion for a directed verdict, which asked that Judge Murphy take the case from the jury and dismiss the charges on the ground that, on the basis of the prosecution evidence, there was nothing to submit to the jury and that as a matter of law, no crime—not murder, not manslaughter, not assault, not even disturbing the peace—had been established by the State.

Though each witness had maintained that there was no provocation by the crowd (estimated variously by the witnesses as between 25 and 150, but actually much larger, as subsequent testimony was to show) the police had admitted finding stones and rocks on the roof and in the yard of the Sweet house after the shooting. There had been no evidence as to who had fired the shot that had killed Leon Breiner, and the cross-examination of officer Gill, who had admitted firing two shots, at least raised the possibility that it was his shot which struck the victim.

Out of the presence of the jury, Hays argued that all the prosecution had proved so far was that there were arms in the house, that there was some shooting from the house, and that the eleven defendants had been in the house. None of this, said Hays, proved a conspiracy on the part of the defendants to murder Leon Breiner or anyone else.

> If there was an agreement of any kind connected with this affair, [he said] the agreement was between Sweet and his friends to protect his property, and the evidence shows that these defendants were there for a lawful purpose. The old principle of a man's right to protect his home as his castle applies directly here.
>
> Every condition in the house was consistent with a lawful purpose. There were no lights because the people in the house feared they would be killed from outside—there was food cooking on the kitchen stove because every man must eat and because none of them could have gone outside the house to obtain food. This whole case stands or falls with the proof or failure to prove a conspiracy to commit murder.

Darrow, in turn, claimed that the State's own witnesses, by their number alone, established that there was a large and hostile crowd outside the Sweet house. "I don't want to say anything to kindle a fire that would be destructive to what civilization Detroit has, but I do think that these defendants were defending themselves from a mob."

In any case, he said, it was easy to say, in the comfort and security of the courtroom, that the defendants had fired too quickly, if indeed there had been evidence, which was not the case, that shots from inside the house hit Breiner. Darrow continued:

A lawful conspiracy can never ripen into crime. There might have been a conspiracy of the defendants to protect the property and lives of some of the eleven. If the prosecution desires to prove conspiracy against one man, it must submit evidence directly against the one man. So far in this trial, there has been no evidence against any one man of the eleven charged.

Only one bullet killed Breiner. Who fired that bullet? The man who fired the shot can only be guilty of manslaughter, but who was that one man? Let the prosecution pick him out.

Prosecutor Toms argued that the killing itself proved the conspiracy, thus indicating why prosecutors have always had a special fondness for conspiracy theories. Conspiracy lightens the burden of proof to featherweight. If several people act in concert and a particular result follows, then the difficult problems of individual culpability can be avoided, if it can be said that the defendants conspired to produce the result and committed some overt acts that contributed to the result.

It is not material, [Toms said] whether the conspiracy was prearranged or entered into at the moment of the crime. The time when the agreement was made is not material so long as it was made sometime before the actual commission of the offense. The agreement may be an instantaneous contract formed under the exigencies of the moment.

The prosecution in this case does not need to show

that the conspirators met and agreed jointly before the alleged crime. The act of any one defendant in any conspiracy in taking life is the act of all. Each conspirator is criminally liable for the acts of all. The existence of a conspiracy should be decided by the jury, and not by the court.

If the court directs a verdict of not guilty in this case, it means that the people of this city, both white and Negro, are notified that it is entirely lawful for two or two hundred of them to gather in a house; to provide weapons in sufficient numbers to arm them all; to fire volleys from the house and to kill one or a dozen under the pretext that they believe themselves to be in danger.

Even Toms was beginning to have second thoughts about at least one of the defendants. He had been bothered, throughout the trial, by the attractive, dignified presence of Mrs. Ossian Sweet in the courtroom and he had sensed sympathy waves passing between her and the jury. Assuming that he got past the motion for a directed verdict (and he could not imagine that a politically conscious judge would risk taking the case away from the jury) he calculated that it would be easier for the jury to find a sinister conspiracy among the defendants without the presence of Mrs. Sweet, a singularly nonsinister person. Ten blacks for one white was a sufficient ratio in any case and, furthermore, the State's evidence had not managed to get Mrs. Sweet out of the kitchen on the night of the shooting.

Accordingly, Toms told Judge Murphy that the State was not opposing the motion as to Mrs. Sweet and suggested that the motion for a directed verdict be granted as to her alone. Immediately Darrow and Hays objected. They were as aware as Toms of Mrs. Sweet's value to the defense and had no real fear that she would be found guilty by the jury, even if all the others were. Their argument to the court, however, was on different grounds. Such a ruling on her behalf alone would be prejudicial to the other defendants, since it could suggest to the jury that though the judge was convinced of Mrs. Sweet's innocence, he entertained doubts as to that of the others.

She is just as guilty or just as innocent as the others, argued Darrow, and either the motion must be granted as to all or denied as to all. When Toms persisted, Darrow said, "If you think her not guilty you should *nolle prosse* the action against her."

An entirely different inference, Darrow knew, would be drawn by the jury if the prosecution admitted that it had no case against her. When Toms refused, Darrow withdrew his motion for a directed verdict in behalf of Mrs. Sweet and let it stand as to the others. Judge Murphy, at that point probably truer to his political instinct than his judicial instinct, then ruled, "I consider it my duty under the evidence submitted to let this case go to the jury." He instructed Darrow and Hays to proceed with their defense.

Arthur Garfield Hays began the opening statement for the defense by asking each member of the Sweet family, including Mrs. Sweet, to stand while he gave a short biographical sketch of each. Then he said to the jury, "These are four of the defendants and the first fact in our case of which we shall expect you gentlemen to take notice is that they don't look like murderers."

Hays then went on to explain the law of self-defense; that one is justified in defending himself when he apprehends that his life is in danger and when that apprehension is reasonable under the circumstances. In this case, Hays said, one of the circumstances that had to be considered, perhaps the most important circumstance, was the color of the defendants:

> The question is not what a white man in a city of whites would do under certain circumstances. The question is what a colored man, a reasonable colored man, with his knowledge of the prejudices against him because of his color; with his knowledge that people have threatened to bomb his home and kill him if he moved into the

neighborhood; with his knowledge that there is a society of man—so-called improvement association—formed for the purpose of ejecting him from his home; with knowledge of what mobs do and have done to colored people when they have had the power; with his knowledge of history, his knowledge of psychology; with his apprehension and fear from the facts as they appear to him.

The first witnesses for the defense immediately painted an entirely different picture of the mood of the crowd at Garland and Charlevoix on September 9. Charles Smith testified that he had been passing through the Garland Avenue district at about 8:00 P.M., and that the car in which he was riding with two other blacks had been bombarded with stones and bricks and that one of the car windows had been broken. The crowd, he said, had spread out over the entire street, slowing the car's pace to five miles per hour.

Alonzo Smith, another passenger in the same car, testified:

Smith: As soon as we struck Charlevoix we saw a crowd. My nephew, who was driving, got curious and drove into it. He came near finding out, too. We heard people yelling, "Here's a nigger now; kill him. He's going to the Sweets."

Darrow: Where was that?

Smith: We had just turned off Charlevoix to St. Clair.

Darrow: Tell us what happened.

Smith: The crowd was dense. I told my nephew to keep going even if he had to run over someone. Edward Smith, who was riding beside my nephew in the front seat, got out on the running board, made off as if he had a gun, and threatened to shoot.

The Smiths estimated the crowd as over one thousand. Though this was probably too high an estimate, it was closer to the truth than the prosecutors' figures. A white newspaperman called by the defense estimated the crowd as in excess of five hundred and was the first witness to testify that he had seen stones thrown at the house. Two other white witnesses testified that stones were thrown, though this was, apparently, about one half hour before the shooting—which they did not witness.

But it was the defendants themselves who would have to provide the testimony which, in the end, would weigh most heavily with the jury. The jurors had been told, from over seventy-five viewpoints, how things had appeared from outside the house. Only the Sweets and their friends could tell how it had looked from inside. In order to justify the taking of a life with the claim of self-defense, it would be necessary to show that the defendants were put in fear of their own lives, and that they had reasonable grounds for that fear. To do that, Darrow and Hays proposed to show the state of mind of the defendants at the moment the shots were fired—a state of mind induced not only by the excitement and panic of the moment but by their life experience of being "separate but equal" blacks in a white country, and by their knowledge of what had been happening to blacks in Detroit in 1925 and indeed what had been happening to blacks in all the history of white America.

Ossian Sweet was the most articulate and the most intelligent of the defendants and so it would be his testimony which would carry the burden of that story. He, in any case, was the principal villain in the eyes of the jury, regardless of who had fired the fatal shot, since in their view, it was his rashness and stubbornness in moving into the neighborhood that had caused all the trouble. Though Sweet was a knowledgeable person with more than an average familiarity with black literature and history, Darrow and Hays were taking no chances. For the past three weeks almost every day after court had adjourned, Ossian Sweet and his lawyers had retired to the Wayne County jail for seminars in what must have been a pioneer black studies program. Using materials supplied by the NAACP, whose Walter White was on hand for the trial, the history of race relations in America was reviewed and Sweet was carefully prepared for his testimony.

In order to lay a foundation for that testimony Darrow first called Walter White, in his official capacity as assistant secretary of the NAACP, to introduce records and reports of that organization on lynching and race riots in the United States. The prosecution objected vigorously to the admission of White's testimony on the basis, first, that it was hearsay evidence unless White had direct knowledge of the incidents he proposed to describe, and second, that the testimony was irrelevant in any case and could have no bearing on the events at Charlevoix and Garland on September 9.

As to the hearsay objection, Darrow argued that, as the witness would testify, the facts, statistics, and reports were required to be kept by White in the regular course of his duties as assistant secretary and were therefore admissible under the business records exception to the hearsay rule, and that in any case the defense did not propose to introduce the records to establish the truth of the facts set forth but merely to show the information that contributed to the defendants' state of mind.

That White's testimony was relevant for that purpose was beyond question, argued Darrow. Just as the members of the Waterworks Improvement Association brought their fears and prejudices to their determination to keep the Sweets out of their house, so did the Sweets bring their fears and prejudices to their determination to defend the house. The case, argued the defense, did not begin with the shooting, or the purchase of the house, but rather began when whites and blacks began to fear and mistrust each other and no one knows when that was or how long it will continue.

The prosecutors argued that this was philosophy, not fact, and courts of law deal in facts. The facts were that Leon Breiner had been killed. The defendants had taken guns and ammunition into the house pursuant to an agreement. Guns are for killing—a killing had ensued. Those were facts—the rest is philosophy. Judge Murphy did not agree. He ruled that Walter White's testimony was admissible for the purpose of introducing data and reports of racial incidents which, if known to the defendants, could have contributed to their state of mind.

Defendants in conspiracy trials are not always so fortunate in our judicial system, which so far has produced more Julius Hoffmans than Frank Murphys. In 1970, in the trial of the so-called Chicago Seven for conspiring to cross state lines to incite a riot at the Democratic Convention in 1968, Judge Hoffman refused to allow defense testimony by a former United States attorney general calculated to show the state of mind of Chicago during that riotous time. The defendants' argument that they were in Chicago to exercise their right of dissent and that they were victims, rather than inciters, of riot simply because they refused to give up that right of dissent did not seem to be an issue to Judge Hoffman. To expect those defendants to give up their right of dissent because the mood of Chicago was ugly should be as insulting to freedom as it was to expect the Sweets to give up their house because the mood of the waterworks improvers was ugly.

And so, Ramsey Clark, who had been attorney general of the United States at the time of the Chicago convention riot, who had taken part in the preconvention planning, who had personally witnessed many of the events, was not allowed to testify in Judge Hoffman's court. Darrow himself made an appearance in the Chicago Trial, thirty-two years after his death. But to Judge Hoffman Darrow was just as unwelcome as Ramsey Clark. When one of the Chicago defense counsel, in closing argument, attempted to quote what Darrow had said in an earlier conspiracy trial in Chicago arising out of a labor dispute in 1896, he was cut off by the judge. This was extraordinary, even by Hoffman standards, since lawyers are always permitted wide latitude in final arguments.

Thirty-five years before, Walter White, who had not even been in Detroit until the critical events were over and who had witnessed none of them, was allowed to testify in Judge Murphy's court. The law of evidence was the same, but the judges were different.

PART IV

XII

Black Pride
and Black Fear

I say that no American citizen unless he is black, need
wait until an angry mob sets foot upon his premises
before he kills. I say that no free man need wait to see
just how far an aggressor will go before he takes life.
The first instinct a man has is to save his life. He doesn't
need to experiment. He hasn't time to experiment. When
he thinks it is time to save his life, he has the right to
act. . . . It has been the law of every English-speaking
country so long as we have had law. Every man's home
is his castle, which even the king may not enter. Every
man has a right to kill to defend himself or his family,
or others, either in defense of the home, or in defense of
themselves. So far as that branch of the case is concerned,
there is only one thing that this jury has a right to consider, and that is whether the defendants acted in honest
fear of danger. That is all. Perhaps they could have
safely waited longer. I know a little about psychology.
If I could talk to a man long enough, and not too long,
and he talks to me a little, I could guess fairly well what
is going on in his head, but I can't understand the
psychology of a mob, and neither can anybody else. We
know it is filled with hatred. We know it is cruel. We
know it has no heart, no soul, and no pity. We know

it is as cruel as the grave. No man has a right to stop and dicker while waiting for a mob.

Walter White testified that, according to the NAACP records, three thousand blacks had been lynched in the United States since the turn of the century. He stated that the Detroit branch had recorded as unjustifiable forty killings of blacks by Detroit policemen since 1923 and that no action, either departmental or criminal, had been taken against any of the policemen involved. He described the revival of the Ku Klux Klan in the past decade and gave a representative sampling of KKK attacks on blacks. He told of the East St. Louis riot, the Washington riot, and the Chicago riot of recent years. He described the 1919 lynching of a black prisoner by a mob of five thousand white Nebraskans who also inflicted fatal wounds on the mayor of Omaha, who had tried to prevent the lynching. Finally, he produced and read from the NAACP records accounts of bombings in the past two years of homes owned by blacks and of attacks on their homes in Detroit during the summer of 1925.

A. Phillip Randolph was urging black resistance and black retaliation to white oppression and even the NAACP, which Randolph considered too moderate, was being goaded to militancy by W. E. B. Du Bois. All over the country blacks were taking pride in the many instances of black war veterans meeting violence with violence. Any new leader who could strike a responsive chord in this new spirit of black America was immediately assured of a large and enthusiastic following. This was dramatized for Sweet by the spectacular career of Marcus Garvey, whose radical proposals had stirred masses of the black working class more than Randolph, the NAACP, or the Urban League had ever been able to do. Garvey had declared that whites would always be racist and oppressive to blacks and that blacks should therefore develop their own culture and racial pride and, though he did not use the phrase, certainly was the first black leader to preach the "black is beautiful" philosophy.

Garvey called his movement the Universal Negro Improvement Association and proposed, as its ultimate goal, the migration of all American blacks to Africa. This part of his program, which, in fact, sent no blacks to Africa, appealed more to whites than to blacks, and eventually led to Garvey's downfall. He founded a steamship company to be used for the great exodus to Africa, but was indicted and convicted for using the mails to defraud in connection with sales of stock in the company. It must, indeed, have required an extraordinary effort by the forces of law and order to send this black man to prison for stock fraud during a period when there were virtually no meaningful securities laws and when stock manipulation and exploitation of the investing public were routine daily work for Wall Street tycoons. When Garvey was released from prison in 1927, he was deported—not to Africa but to the British West Indies, where he had been born.

Ossian Sweet, though he had no interest in Africa, had been moved, as were most blacks, by Garvey's passionate calls for black pride and black identity, and though he had always thought that he had never wanted anything more than to get along in the world by playing the game according to the white man's rules, he began to look upon himself as the leader of more than just the eleven people in the courtroom. The image of a terrified black man quivering with fear might save eleven, but might also be a betrayal of eleven million. The fear that he had experienced on September 9 had been forgotten and he now felt only pride and defiance. That, he told Darrow and Hays, was what he wanted to express from the witness stand.

Darrow, of course, could sympathize with Sweet's position. What he and Hays were asking Sweet to do was like asking John Brown to apologize for Harpers Ferry. But Darrow's job was to keep the defendants out of prison and that job might have to be accomplished at the expense of black pride. Darrow told Sweet that it would be difficult enough for this white jury to understand and forgive a black man's act done out of reaction to fear; what a white jury would never tolerate would be a black man's defiance. Darrow pointed out that the cause of blacks everywhere would be advanced by an acquittal, whereas a conviction would be a signal to whites that they were free to continue intimidation and harrassment of blacks.

In the end, Sweet agreed to the humble approach and Darrow promised that in his final argument he would not apologize for the shooting or seek forgiveness of it but would defend and justify it. The jury, Darrow told Sweet, would not resent that attitude when expressed by a white man so long as they could continue to feel a moral superiority to the black man in the dock. As always, the black man was forced to play the game according to the white man's rules. Sweet played his part well. The *Free Press* reported on November 20:

> Dr. Ossian H. Sweet, on trial with his wife and nine other Negroes for killing, figuratively opened the doors of his Garland Avenue home in Judge Frank Murphy's courtroom Thursday and showed the fright, the hysteria, the bedlam within the house the night Leon Breiner met his death from a shot fired from within the Sweet home.

Hays carefully and skillfully had directed Sweet in a recital of his life, emphasizing the points at which that life had been touched with incidents of racial violence and intimidation. He told of the burning of eighteen black homes, one black church, and the killing of five blacks in the small town of Rosewood, outside of Orlando, where Sweet had been born. He told how he had seen a black man pulled from a streetcar and beaten by a white mob during the Washington riots. He told of the killing of Mrs. Mitchell's brother during the Chicago riots, and how he had read and been deeply affected by accounts of lynchings and racial incidents all over the country in the past five years. Hays then shifted the scene to Detroit and had Sweet describe the Turner incident and his knowledge of the other attacks on blacks that summer, his purchase of the house, and the subsequent threats against him and Mrs. Smith. He freely admitted the purchase of the guns and ammunition and described the events of September 8 and September 9 up to that evening. And then:

Q: When did you first observe anything outside?

A: We were playing cards; it was about eight o'clock when something hit the roof of the house.

Q: What happened after that?

A: Somebody went to the window and shouted, "The people, the people."

Q: And then?

A: I ran out to the kitchen where my wife was; there were several lights burning; I turned them out, and opened the door. I heard someone yell: "Go and raise hell in front, I'm going back."

Q: What happened then?

A: Pandemonium—I guess that's the best way of describing it—broke loose. Everyone was running from room to room. There was a general uproar. Somebody yelled, "There's someone coming!" They said, "That's your brother." A car had pulled up to the curb. My brother and Mr. Davis got out. The mob yelled, "Here's niggers! Get them, get them." As they rushed in, the mob surged forward fifteen or twenty feet. It looked like a human sea. Stones kept coming faster. I ran downstairs. Another window was smashed. Then one shot then eight or ten from upstairs, then it was all over.

The rest of Sweet's testimony dealt with the arrival of the police, the search of the house, and the arrest of the defendants. He said that on the way to the police station one of the officers had asked him why he had moved into a white neighborhood when he knew he was not wanted. His answer was that there was nowhere else to move.

Over the prosecution's objection Hays then asked Sweet to describe his state of mind at the time of the shooting:

When I opened the door and saw the mob, I realized I
was facing the same mob that had hounded my people
throughout its entire history. In my mind I was pretty
confident of what I was up against, with my back
against the wall. I was filled with a peculiar fear, the
kind no one could feel unless they had known the history of our race. I knew what mobs had done to my
people before.

In the statement which Sweet had given the police on the
night of the shooting he had said that he had gone to his
room to lie down at about 8:00 P.M. and had not left the room
till after the shooting. He had said that his nerves were undone
and he knew from his medical training that rest might settle
them. On cross-examination Toms immediately attacked Sweet
for the inconsistencies between that statement and his testimony. "I am under oath now," said Sweet. "I was very excited
then and I was afraid that anything I said might be misin-
terpreted."

When Toms persisted, Darrow interrupted to say that the
trial would be expedited if it were agreed, as the defense
admitted, that Sweet's statement to the police that night was
untrue in most of its details. This concession took most of the
steam out of Tom's cross-examination and he was not able to
change Sweet's story in any material respect despite five hours
of cross-examination. Toms questioned Sweet closely about his
fear of mob violence. He asked him about the source of his
information as to the danger of a Negro being lynched in
Michigan. Quoting one of the NAACP reports which listed
only four lynchings in Michigan in the twentieth century, Toms
asked Sweet if he had read the report. Sweet replied that he
had and then Toms asked why he feared lynching when the
last event of that kind had taken place several years ago and
the last man lynched had been white. Sweet answered, "I
thought that if Michigan mobs could find Negroes to lynch
when there were comparatively few here that there was a good
deal of danger now that there are 80,000 of us."

Ossian Sweet was the only one of the defendants to testify and, after some rebuttal by police officers who were permitted to read into the record the defendants' statements given the night of the shooting, the case of *The People of the State of Michigan* v. *Ossian Sweet, et al.* was ready for final argument.

XIII

Cold-Blooded
Murderers

Who are these people who were in this house? Were they
people of character? Were they people of standing? Were
they people of intelligence? First, there was Dr. Sweet.
Gentlemen, a white man does pretty well when he does
what Dr. Sweet did. But, Dr. Sweet has the handicap of the
color of his face. . . .

Who are these men who were in this house? —Were
they hoodlums? Were they criminals? Were they anything except men who asked for a chance to breathe the
free air and make their own way, earn their own living,
and get their bread by the sweat of their brow? . . .

Gentlemen, these black men shot. Whether any bullets
from their guns hit Breiner, I do not care, I will not
discuss it. It is passing strange that the bullet that went
through him, went directly through, and not as if it was
shot from some higher place. It was not the bullet that
came from Henry Sweet's rifle, that is plain. It might have
come from the house; I do not know, gentlemen, and I do
not care. There are bigger issues in this case than that.
The right to defend your person is as sacred a right as any
human being could fight for, and as sacred a cause as any
jury could sustain. That issue not only involves the defendants in this case, it involves every man who wants to

live, every man who wants freedom to work and to breathe; it is an issue worth fighting for, and worth dying for, it is an issue worth the attention of this jury, who have had a chance that is given to few juries to pass upon a real case that will mean something in the history of a race.

The trial was almost a month old and the temper of Detroit had changed considerably since it had begun. The reelection of John Smith as mayor during the first week of the trial had kept the Ku Klux Klan out of City Hall and had emboldened Smith to call again for understanding and harmony between the races. The Detroit newspapers decidedly hostile at the outset, had been won over by Darrow's and Hays' conduct of the trial, and Judge Murphy's calm and firm control of the proceedings had contributed greatly to the lessening of tensions. The favorable reports in the newspapers of the defense witnesses' demeanor and testimony, in contrast to that of most of the prosecution witnesses, had caused Darrow and Hays to think that public sympathy was shifting toward the defendants. Detroit no longer seemed to be a city in the grip of fear. This was important to the argument that Darrow and Hays had determined to make. In order to gain an acquittal, it was going to be necessary to attack the integrity of the Detroit Police Department and attacking police is never popular in a society obsessed with law and order. Detroit seemed less obsessed at the end of November than it had been at the end of October.

Though the civilian prosecution witnesses had wavered on cross-examination, all the police witnesses had persistently maintained that there had been no threat to the Sweets' safety and that the Sweets could not reasonably have felt threatened by anything that occurred in the streets before the shooting.

If the jury was to believe the defendants, they would also have to believe that the police either lied or were terribly mistaken. Darrow did not give them the benefit of the doubt:

> It is my conviction that every one of the witnesses for the State perjured himself time and time again in this case. There was not an honest person in the whole bunch. . . .
>
> There isn't an officer in this case who isn't partly guilty of the crime and who hasn't committed perjury to protect himself. And this doesn't necessarily mean that they are bad, but they are victims of an instinctive hatred of anything which appears as social equality of the black race, that they are willing to perjure themselves for what they conceive of as their superb nordic race. . . .
>
> That's what I am afraid of, gentlemen. . . . If I thought any of you men had any opinion about the guilt of my clients I wouldn't worry, because that might be changed. What I am worried about is your prejudices. They are harder to change. They come with your mother's milk and stick like the color of skin. . . .
>
> My clients are charged with murder but they are really here because they are black.

Darrow returned again and again to the police:

> This superintendent came and looked over the ground like a great general on the eve of a battle. Except that he wasn't a great general though this was a battle. . . .
>
> I tell you these policemen were no good. They lied and were evidently in league with this glorious league, this Waterworks Improvement Association. . . .
>
> I say that a man who has been on the police force thirty years and who comes here as your assistant commissioner and swears that there was no crowd at the Sweet house is not to be trusted. He lies.

The main thrust of Darrow's argument, aside from his attack on the prosecution witnesses and especially the police, was an appeal to the jury to lay aside their prejudices. Darrow's arguments were always a blend of history, psychology, and phi-

losophy and almost always contained the recitation of a poem
if he could find one reasonably relevant. He sometimes claimed
that this was the influence of Edgar Lee Masters, who, early
in the century, was Darrow's law partner in Chicago. This may
have been so but the *Spoon River Anthology* never found its
way into a Darrow summation.

The poem this time was by Countee Cullen, a popular black
poet of the day. Darrow had not been neglecting his black
studies program.

> Once riding in old Baltimore,
> Heart full, head full of glee
> I saw a Baltimorean
> Stand gazing there at me.
>
> Now, I was eight and very small
> And he was no whit bigger,
> And so I smiled, but he stuck out
> His tongue and called me nigger.
>
> I saw the whole of Baltimore
> From April till December,
> Of all the things that I saw there
> That's all that I remember.

Darrow closed his argument by saying:

> The Sweets spent their first night in their first home
> afraid to go to bed. The next night they spent in jail.
> Now the State wants them to spend the rest of their
> lives in the penitentiary. The State claims that there was
> no mob there that night. Gentlemen, the State has put
> on enough witnesses who said they were there, to make
> a mob.
>
> There are persons in the North and South who say a
> black man is inferior to the white and should be con-
> trolled by the whites. There are also those who recog-
> nize his rights and say he should enjoy them. To me this
> case is a cross-section of human history; it involves the
> future, and the hope of some of us that the future shall
> be better than the past.

The case went to the jury on the day before Thanksgiving, after a rebuttal argument by Toms and the charge to the jury by Judge Murphy. Almost immediately there were rumors that bitter arguments were taking place in the jury room. Jury security was apparently less than perfect in Recorders Court and courthouse attendants reported that on the first vote a majority of the jurors had been for conviction of at least some of the defendants.

The last words to the jury had belonged to the prosecution and they had been strong words. Toms said:

> Back of all your sophistry and transparent political philosophy, gentlemen of the defense, back of all your prating of civil rights, back of your psychology and theory of race hatred, lies the stark body of Leon Breiner with a bullet hole in his back. Bury it if you will or if you can, beneath an avalanche of copies of the *Crisis*, or the *Defender*, or the *Independent*, or reports of committees and commissions in other cities, still out from under the avalanche peers the mute face of Leon Breiner, its lips silent forever.
>
> All your specious arguments, Mr. Darrow, all your artful ingenuity born of years of experience—all of your social theories, Mr. Hays; all your cleverly conceived psychology can never dethrone justice in this case. Leon Breiner, peacefully chatting with his neighbor at his doorstep enjoying his God-given and inalienable right to live, is shot through the back from ambush. And you can't make anything out of these facts, gentlemen of the defense, but cold-blooded murder.

The sting of those words was somewhat lessened by Judge Murphy's charge, which was fair and reasonable, and, if anything, weighted toward the defendants. He removed the conspiracy theory from the jury's consideration by directing them that only those defendants whose overt acts indicated individual responsibility could be found guilty. On the evidence submitted this limited the guilty possibilities to Ossian and Henry Sweet: Ossian, for directing and controlling the operation, and Henry, because he was the only one of the defendants who admitted firing his gun. Though Henry had not testified, the prosecution had been permitted to read into evidence his statement given on the night of the shooting. No witness for the State had been able to say which of the defendants had fired the shots and Ossian had claimed not to know who had done the shooting. None of the defendants could be found guilty, Murphy said, if the jury found that the force used by them in defense of the house was reasonable under the circumstances, including the state of mind of the defendants at the time of the shooting.

The NAACP, which was not accustomed to such even-handed treatment in or out of court, was duly impressed. *Crisis* reported:

> Seldom in any court has a more impartial, learned or complete charge to a jury been heard. As was evidenced throughout the case, Judge Murphy was exerting every effort at his command to assure to the eleven defendants a completely fair trial. His charge to the jury reached its dramatic climax when in a voice filled with emotion and sincerity, he declared, "Dr. Sweet has the same right under the law to purchase and occupy the dwelling house on Garland Avenue as any other man. Under the law, a man's house is his castle. It is his castle, whether he is white or black, and no man has the right to assail or invade it. . . .

All day long rumors flew through the courthouse—11 to 1 for acquittal, 10 to 2 for conviction. Angry shouts were heard from time to time inside the jury room. At midnight word came that the jury wanted clarification of part of the judge's instructions, and that portion of the charge dealing with self-defense was read again to the jury. At 2:00 A.M. the jury, still without a verdict, was put to bed for the night.

The next day, Thanksgiving, deliberations were interrupted for a turkey dinner. The *Free Press* reported:

Though Thanksgiving day can hardly have been an ideal one for the 12 jurors, the city did not overlook them. A splendid turkey dinner with fixings was ordered for them. Everything is being done for their comfort consistent with segregation from the rest of the world.

The defendants, of course, were also segregated from the rest of the world, in the Wayne County Jail. Their Thanksgiving dinner menu was not reported.

The turkey fixings failed to produce any unanimity among the jurors and at midnight they again retired. At 1:30 P.M. the next afternoon the jury reported to the court that it was hopelessly deadlocked, and Judge Murphy declared a mistrial and dismissed the jury. Darrow and Hays, at the outset of the trial, would have gladly settled for a hung jury but the changing mood they sensed during the trial had, by the end of it, encouraged them to expect a verdict of acquittal for at least some of the defendants. As it turned out, at the time the jury gave up the vote appeared to be 10 to 2 for acquittal of all the defendants except Henry and Ossian Sweet and the final count on them was 7 to 5 for conviction—but for manslaughter instead of murder.

This information, of course, was not part of the court record and, in fact, some of the jurors were unwilling to talk about their deliberations. But the consensus of those who made statements indicated it was the unshakable racial fear of two jurors, who went into the case as bigots and came out of the case as bigots, that prevented a verdict.

Regardless of the form of the verdict, Darrow expected that the charges would be dropped against the defendants and though it had not been a clear-cut affirmation by a white jury of the right of a black man to shoot a white man in self-defense, it had come close enough to at least act as a warning to white mobs. But to Darrow's surprise, shock, and disgust, prosecutor Toms immediately announced that the charges against the defendants would not be dismissed and that the state of Michigan would try them all again for murder. White Detroit had not yet been avenged.

XIV

Forget and Forgive

Gentlemen, I feel deeply on this subject; I cannot help
it. Let us take a little glance at the history of the Negro
race. It only needs a minute. It seems to me that the story
would melt hearts of stone. . . . Their ancestors were
captured in the jungles and in the plains of Africa, captured as you capture wild beasts, torn from their homes
and their kindred; loaded into slave ships, packed like
sardines in a box, half of them dying on the ocean
passage; some jumping into the sea in their frenzy, when
they had a chance to choose death in the place of
slavery. . . . They were bought and sold as slaves, to
work without pay, because they were black. They were
subjected to all this for generations, until finally they
were given their liberty so far as the law goes—and that
is only a little way, because, after all, every human being's
life in this world is inevitably mixed with every other life
and, no matter what laws we pass, no matter what pre-
cautions we take, unless the people we meet are kindly
and decent and human and liberty-loving, then there is
no liberty.

Darrow immediately applied to have the defendants released
on bail. All except Mrs. Sweet had been in jail for almost

three months and it was not expected that the retrial could be held before spring. Toms agreed to bail for all except Ossian and Henry Sweet. Darrow pointed out that those two were the ones least likely to fail to appear for trial and hence the best subjects for bail. But Toms, as prosecutors like to do, was using bail as a punishment tool and, since he considered Ossian and Henry Sweet the most culpable, resisted bail for them. Judge Murphy compromised and ordered all the prisoners except Ossian and Henry released on $5,000 bail. For the Sweet brothers bail was set at $10,000. Bonds for each defendant were promptly furnished by sources provided by the NAACP.

Ossian Sweet did not attempt to move back into the house on Garland and joined his wife and baby at Mrs. Mitchell's house on Kearney Street. The deserted Sweet house, which must have been a mocking reminder to the waterworks improvers, was set on fire one night that winter. The blaze was extinguished without extensive damage and the house was put under police guard.

Darrow returned to Detroit early in April, 1926, to prepare for the second trial, which was scheduled to begin on April 19. Hays, who was involved in another case at that time, did not take part in the retrial. Darrow was assisted instead by Thomas Chawke and Julian Perry, black lawyers from Detroit. Toms and Moll again appeared for the prosecution. Darrow had moved for separate trials for each of the defendants and the State elected to try Henry Sweet since he was the only one who had admitted firing any shots. Darrow had instructed his investigators to knock on every door in Detroit, if necessary, in order to find more people who might be willing to tell the truth about what had happened on September 9. He used the intervening time himself to prepare a more thorough examination and argument. He had had only a week's preparation before the first trial and he was determined that the second trial should have a more satisfactory result.

Darrow was not unhappy to be back in Detroit. He enjoyed the good feeling of being able to go across the river to

Windsor, Ontario, for a legal drink of liquor. He liked to compare his flight for a drink to the slave's flight for freedom:

> Even before the Civil War the runaway slaves would come to Detroit, for this city was in sight of the Union Jack which was flying beyond the river, in Windsor, Canada. To the footsore slave fleeing from his master, the Union Jack was the emblem of freedom, just as today it is for the thirsty.

Furthermore, he enjoyed the extra satisfaction that a lawyer takes in his work if he likes and respects his clients and believes absolutely in their cause. And Darrow also looked forward to trying another case before Judge Murphy, whom he considered to be a superior judge in every respect. He was fortunate to have found these extra gratifications in the Sweet case, because his fee was only a fraction of what he ordinarily charged for a comparable case—$5,000—a sum which he nevertheless considered much more satisfying than the $30,000 he had finally received for the Loeb–Leopold case.

With the new witnesses they had been able to find during their investigation, and with the extra time for preparation, Darrow was confident of an acquittal, which would surely be followed by a dismissal against the other defendants. If the State could not secure a conviction against Henry Sweet, against whom the prosecution had its only solid evidence, it would have no chance against the others. Even the most vengeful prosecutor would have to know that.

Once again, Darrow considered whether or not the jury should be waived. Two years before, in Chicago, Darrow had waived a jury in the Loeb–Leopold case under very special circumstances. The defendants had confessed to the wanton and motiveless killing of a young boy and Darrow had no alternative but to plead them guilty and then, to save their lives, have a trial on the sole issue of mitigation. Under Illinois law the defendants were entitled to a jury trial on that issue and Darrow had calculated that if twelve jurors could divide the responsibility of sending these two killers to their deaths they would do it gladly, but a judge, bearing the sole responsibility, might settle for life imprisonment. Darrow won that gamble and would have been willing to gamble again with Judge Murphy. He told Ossian Sweet and Henry that he was almost certain he could secure an acquittal from Judge Murphy and less than certain that result would follow a jury trial. But, he told them, the advantages to be gained from a jury acquittal far outweighed the risk of another hung jury. The danger of a guilty verdict he viewed as minimal. A jury verdict of acquittal would vindicate everything they and the NAACP had fought for and could be of great importance in liberating blacks from the kind of white oppression that was keeping blacks crowded together in Paradise Valleys and Blackbottoms all over the country. The Sweets agreed that the case should be tried before a jury.

The second trial was much like the first. Again the prosecution witnesses paraded to the stand with the same incredible stories concerning the size and conduct of the crowd on September 9. But this time, armed with a better investigation, the cross-examinations were more searching and fruitful, and the defense had found three more white witnesses who estimated the crowd as in excess of three hundred and characterized that crowd as far from friendly and orderly. Darrow was less gentle this time with the prosecution witnesses and did not hesitate to let the jury know that, in his view, the Sweets were moving into a neighborhood where they would be among their inferiors. He was particularly hard on a prosecution witness who lived on Goethe Street but had difficulty pronouncing it. Darrow had sneered at her for being too cultivated to accept black neighbors but too ignorant to pronounce *Goethe* correctly. He later wrote:

> The trial revealed a marked contrast between the Klansmen and other witnesses for the State, and the colored defendants and their friends who testified for our side. Practically all the Negroes who came upon the stand were men and women of culture and refinement,

many college graduates, and in every way the superiors of the witnesses for the prosecution.

Toms had been concerned with the medical testimony at the first trial which left open the possibility that the fatal shot had been fired from street level and Henry Sweet had admitted firing shots only from the second floor. In order to make Sweet's shots consistent with the nature of Breiner's wound the prosecutor had prepared extensive medical and ballistic testimony. But Darrow did not want to make this the issue in the case. If the jury felt that Henry Sweet's guilt or innocence depended upon whether or not the fatal shot came from his gun, it would be too easy for them to find that it did. Darrow readily conceded in open court that the bullet might have been fired by Sweet, and that if it had, it was in defense of his life and home.

The trial followed virtually the same scenario, but this time Henry Sweet, as well as Ossian, took the stand. He made a good witness. Darrow later summarized his testimony:

> Henry was about twenty years old, and had just completed his junior year at Wilberforce College, in Ohio. The evidence was plain that he had shot out of the front window in the direction of the deceased. Henry was very fond of his elder brother, the doctor, who had helped him while attending school. He was really a member of the family, and what he had done was naturally in defense of his brother and kinsfolk, and his race. Even though he might have been hasty in shooting, he was justified in doing so if he believed that the home and the inmates were in danger. Henry made an excellent appearance in the witness chair. He was frank and open-mannered and made no attempt to conceal his part in the tragedy.

In a little over three weeks Darrow again rose for his final argument. It was not only a defense of Henry Sweet, but a defense of Darrow's own philosophy and life. Darrow himself considered it to be "one of the strongest and most satisfactory arguments that I ever delivered." One courtroom observer later said:

> I shall never forget that final plea to the jury. He talked for eight hours. . . . He went back through the pages of history and the progress of the human race to trace the development of fear and prejudice in human psychology. Sometimes his resonant melodious voice sank to a whisper. Sometimes it rose in a roar of indignation. The collars of the jurors wilted. They sat tense, in the grip of . . . historic events and tragic happenings which he made real and present again before their very eyes.

Judge Murphy, who had heard hundreds of lawyers and was to hear hundreds more, said to a friend immediately after the summation, "This is the greatest experience of my life. That was Clarence Darrow at his best. I will never hear anything like it again." Darrow closed his argument by making a plea to the jury, to the generation and to the future:

> Now, gentlemen, just one more word, and I am through with this case. . . . I may not be true to my ideals always, but I believe in the law of love, and I believe you can do nothing with hatred. I would like to see a time when man loves his fellowman, and forgets his color or his creed. We will never be civilized until that time comes. I know the Negro race has a long road to go, I believe the life of the Negro race has been a life of tragedy, of injustice, of oppression. The law has made him equal but man has not, and, after all the last analysis is, what has man done?—and not what has the law done? I know there is a long road ahead of him, before he can take the place which I believe he shall take. I know that before him there is suffering, sorrow, tribulation and death among the blacks, and perhaps the whites. I am sorry. I would do what I could to avert it; I would advise patience; I would advise toleration;

I would advise understanding; I would advise all of those things which are necessary for men who live together.

On May 19, 1926, after deliberating for only four hours (instead of the forty-six hours of the first trial), the jury returned with its verdict of not guilty. In the immediate flush of victory there was a great tendency to attribute too much to the triumph. Darrow at first claimed only one small step forward: "The verdict meant simply that the doctrine that a man's house is his castle applied to the black man as well as the white man. If not the first time that a white jury had vindicated this principle, it was the first that ever came to my notice."

This was true enough, but a month later his optimism had grown and he told the NAACP that he thought the case had marked a turning point in relations between the races and that it could be the beginning of the end of prejudice and bigotry in this country. Less than one year later, on March 11, 1927, Darrow realized how wrong he had been. He himself was almost attacked by a racially inflamed white mob in Mobile, Alabama, which broke up a meeting on race relations being addressed by him at the Lyric Theater. He was forced to leave the meeting hall under police protection. He then went across town and urged a black audience to be more defiant of white oppression.

Du Bois' comment in the *Crisis* on the Sweet verdict was even more optimistic:

> We are not sure that even in their rejoicing most colored Americans appreciate the significance of the acquittal of Henry Sweet. The eleven defendants in Detroit were doomed. The police deliberately lied. Many of the witnesses for the prosecution lied. This was evident to every honest onlooker. The newspapers were prejudiced and biased and the prosecution attorney stooped to appeal to the worst racial antipathies of the community.

This was the pattern that had been repeated in thousands of cases against blacks, said Du Bois, and America's prisons were full of blacks just as innocent as the Sweets. But the difference this time was that the defendants refused to be intimidated; the NAACP was willing to pay the dollar cost of justice in America, and in Clarence Darrow they had found a white man bold enough and skillful enough to dramatize the issue of racism in America and to challenge white America to change its racist attitudes. "This was the combination that won in Detroit," said Du Bois, "and this is the combination that is going to help us carve out wide futures."

But attitudes born of two hundred years of racism do not die so easily. White Detroit, far from conceding that a great social victory had been won, would not even concede that the courtroom battle had been won. To Darrow's amazement the State refused to dismiss the murder charges against the other ten defendants and the charge of shooting with intent to kill Erik Haugberg, which had been pending against all eleven.

Darrow realized that he had misgauged the depth of white hostility at every step along the way. He knew he had been right when he had said that a white man would never have been charged with a crime under similar circumstances but he could understand white fears and he could tolerate white foolishness. He had seen a lot of foolishness in his lifetime. He had been disappointed when bail had been refused his clients but he knew that Detroit, at the time, was a fear-filled city and it was not the first time that victims of injustice had to suffer further injustice in order to avert violence. He had been disappointed when Judge Murphy had refused to direct a verdict in favor of the defendants but he could understand political pressure and political ambition. He had been disappointed when the first jury had failed to reach a verdict of acquittal but he had taken some comfort in the fact that out of twelve white men in a Ku Klux Klan—ridden city only one or two were so blinded with hate they could not see their clear duty.

His patience had worn thin when the State had refused to

dismiss the charges after the first trial, but that was not the first time that he had had to retry a case and he had not been entirely satisfied with the first trial. And at this point he realized that white society still did not feel avenged and perhaps never would for the threat to its security that black defiance represented. Darrow argued bitterly that the prosecution was using the pending charges as some kind of sinister threat to the defendants to extract from them the kind of behavior that whites demanded from blacks. He charged that Toms had no intention of bringing any of the other defendants to trial because he knew he could never get a conviction and he demanded that all charges be dismissed against all defendants. Toms denied that was his purpose and claimed the State simply had not yet made a decision on a trial for the other defendants.

Toms' indecision lasted for more than a year. Finally on July 21, 1927, he filed his motion to dismiss all charges against all the defendants and they were free at last. They had, of course, been out on bail since December, 1925, but the bail bonds and cash securities remained on file and they were technically under arrest and subject to prosecution at any time. What Toms said in his dismissal motion proved two things: one, that Darrow had been absolutely right when he accused Toms of using the pending charges as black intimidation, and two, that Toms was sadly mistaken in his estimate of the future of racial harmony in Detroit.

In his motion filed before Judge Murphy, Toms said:

> This case was first tried against all the defendants jointly. The trial occupied about twenty-five days and the jury, after forty-eight hours [*sic*] disagreed. The case was later retried against Henry Sweet, one of the defendants, alone, the trial occupying about three weeks. The jury after deliberating about three-and-a-half hours, returned a verdict of not guilty as to that defendant. The proofs on behalf of the State as to the defendant Henry Sweet were of greater weight than

the proofs against any other defendant, for example: the defendant both in an extrajudicial statement and as a witness in his own behalf testified that he fired in the direction of the deceased. This cannot be shown of any other defendant.

The prosecuting attorney feels that if the jury in the trial of Henry Sweet was not convinced of his guilt by the evidence produced by the State, a jury trying any of the other defendants against whom the evidence would be far less conclusive, would undoubtedly do likewise. The State has no proof to offer in addition to that produced upon the two former trials and that proof was insufficient in both cases to convince the jury of the defendants' guilt beyond a reasonable doubt.

All of this was true on May 19, 1926, the date of the not-guilty verdict, and Toms knew it. As Darrow had insisted, the cases should have been dismissed then, and would have, had the defendants been white. But, as Darrow pointed out, it is rare for a black man to receive justice in court, whether he wins or loses. The balance of Toms' motion states the real reason for delaying dismissal for over another year:

It is significant that since the trial of this case there has not been a single so-called interracial clash in the city of Detroit and a noticeably improved spirit of tolerance and forbearance has arisen between the colored and white groups in this city. The defendant Ossian Sweet has not attempted to occupy the residence at the corner of Garland Avenue and Charlevoix Street and has offered the same for sale.

In other words, though the verdict of acquittal meant, according to Toms, that there could be no conviction of any of the defendants, he found Ossian Sweet guilty of owning a house and sentenced him to a kind of probation pending his good behavior—the good behavior being the abandonment of his right to live in his house. The waterworks improvers had won, after all.

The new spirit of racial tolerance and of forbearance in Detroit that had been so encouraging to Toms improved so much that in 1943 open warfare broke out between blacks and whites. Detroit, in the early forties, had been swelled by another wave of black and white Southerners drawn north by high-paying defense jobs. The pattern of 1920 was repeated. Blacks and whites worked together on the assembly lines but they could neither live together nor play together. On June 20, fist fights broke out between black and white teen-agers at the Belle Isle amusement park. The fighting escalated to a full-blown and bloody riot, centering first in the same Paradise Valley from which Ossian Sweet had tried to escape twenty years before. By the time federal troops were able to restore order nine whites and twenty-five blacks were dead and two million dollars' worth of property had been destroyed.

The truce lasted only until July, 1967, when the hostility which had existed for forty years between the Detroit police and the city's black citizens erupted into what became the country's bloodiest and costliest (so far) racial violence.

The 1967 riot followed a series of police raids on so-called blind pigs in black ghettoes—after-hours drinking and gambling spots (formerly prohibition speakeasies). The last blind pig raided, on Twelfth Street and Clairmount, was crowded with eighty-two patrons when the police arrived at 3:45 A.M. (a favorite time of day for police raids on black establishments). A crowd of several hundred quickly gathered on the street as the police began arresting the customers. This black neighborhood on this hot July morning was not in a mood hospitable to white policemen. Within the past month two incidents in the Twelfth Street area had inflamed the district to the boiling point. A Negro prostitute had been killed by a vice squad officer, according to the community, and by a pimp, according to the police. A short time later, a twenty-seven-year-old black army veteran had been killed by a gang of white youths. The city's major newspapers had played down the incident but the local black paper had complained of a double standard of news coverage and had reported in great detail how Danny Thomas had been killed in sight of his wife by a white gang shouting, "Niggers keep out of Rouge Park."

One suspect had been arrested, but though the identity of the entire gang was apparently known to the police, no others had been arrested. What, asked the black community, would have been the result if a white man had been killed by a gang of blacks? That question had been answered in Detroit in 1925. One white killed, possibly by accident, and eleven blacks arrested for first-degree murder. Darrow had asked the question in reverse then and his answer had been that the whites would not have been arrested, they would have been given medals, instead. No medals for the killers of Danny Thomas, but not very much law enforcement either (nor have there been medals for the three white policemen who were charged and acquitted of the murder of three black teen-agers at the Algiers Motel in Detroit in the 1967 riot, but the officers have become heroes to the Detroit Police Officers Association and to much of Detroit's white community).

The Thomas family lived only a few blocks from the raided blind pig and in a few hours more than three thousand blacks were out on Twelfth Street and the riot was under way. Six days later it had burned itself out—forty-three deaths, thirty-three black, ten white, and fifty million dollars in property damages. One of the shootings occurred at the corner of Charlevoix and Goethe, one block away from Garland and Charlevoix, deep in the heart of the territory of the long-forgotten Waterworks Improvement Association.

The association had not survived the Sweet trials and several black families had, in fact, moved into the neighborhood shortly after the trials. Sweet was not able to find a buyer willing to pay a fair price for the house and in 1928 he moved back in with his family. He did not live long enough to see a different kind of mob swarm through the neighborhood in July, 1967. Sweet's second stay in his house was longer but not happier than the first. Within two years both his wife and his child died from tuberculosis. He married and divorced two other women but had no children with either. His profes-

sional life continued to be successful though his personal life
was marred by ill fortune.

Shortly after the dismissal of the charges against him in
1927, Leon Breiner's widow sued Sweet for $150,000, claiming
that he had wrongfully caused the death of her husband. The
suit was eventually dismissed but Sweet always believed that
the additional stress of a civil suit after two criminal trials
hastened the death of his wife.

His name became one of the best known in Detroit's black
community and in 1932 he won the Republican primary for
his state senate district but lost to a white man in the general
election. In the thirties he founded and became superintendent
of the Good Samaritan Hospital and bought a prosperous
pharmacy. The Detroit police apparently had not forgotten
Dr. Sweet and in 1934 he was arrested on a warrant charging
him with the sale of cigarettes in his pharmacy without a
license. The charge brought a two-dollar fine and a large
headline in the *Free Press* as though as to say "This fellow
Sweet is causing trouble again."

Following his second divorce in 1944, Sweet sold the house
at Garland and Charlevoix and lived alone the rest of his life.
He again sought public office in 1950 when he ran in the
Democratic primary for Congress. The district in which he
lived had become predominantly black but when another
black candidate entered the race the Negro vote was split
and the incumbent congressman was reelected. Sweet claimed
that the other black had been paid to enter the race by the
incumbent and issued a bitter statement after the primary:
"People who sell out and allow themselves to be used as tools
to continue the disfranchisement of my people and the working classes are traitors to the American way of life."

Ossian Sweet withdrew from public life and became a vir-
tual recluse in the last years of his life. His brother Henry, who
had become a lawyer, had died in 1940 and after 1950 Ossian
saw fewer and fewer people aside from his brother Otis. On
March 19, 1960, alone, despondent, and suffering severely
from arthritis, Ossian Sweet committed suicide by shooting

himself in the head with a 32-caliber revolver. Ossian Sweet, who had always believed in "the American way of life," chose to end his own by gunfire—the American way of death. Otis Sweet continued to practice dentistry until his office was destroyed in the 1967 riots. Whatever memories Otis Sweet has of the events of 1925 he keeps to himself. Now over seventy and retired he says only: "I don't think much about it anymore. You forget and forgive."

XV

A Bundle of Prejudices

Now, gentlemen, I say you are prejudiced. . . . But they tell me there is no race prejudice and it is plain nonsense, and nothing else. Who are we, anyway? A child is born into this world without any knowledge of any sort. He has a brain which is a piece of putty; he inherits nothing in the way of knowledge or ideas. If he is white he knows nothing about color. He has no antipathy to the black. The black and the white both will live together and play together, but as soon as the baby is born we begin giving him ideas. We begin planting seeds in his mind. We begin telling him he must do this and he must not do that. We tell him about race and social equality and the thousands of things that men talk about until he grows up. It has been trained into us, and you, gentlemen, bring that feeling into this jury box, and that feeling which is a part of your life-long training. You need not tell me you are not prejudiced. I know better. We are not very much but a bundle of prejudices anyhow. We are prejudiced against other people's color. Prejudiced against other men's religion; prejudiced against other people's politics. Prejudiced against peoples' looks. Prejudiced about the way we dress. We are full of prejudices. You can teach a man anything beginning with the child;

you can make anything out of him, and we are not responsible for it. Here and there some of us haven't any prejudices on some questions, but if you look deep enough you will find them and we all know it. All I hope for, gentlemen of the jury, is this: That you are strong enough, and honest enough, and decent enough to lay it aside in this case and decide it as you ought to.

After the Sweet trials Clarence Darrow decided, once again, to retire from active practice. He had invested what money he had been able to save in securities and the bull market of the 1920s expanded his capital to the point where he believed he could devote his time to travel, lecturing, and writing. For two years he did so, but the stock market crash of 1929 took all his savings and at the age of seventy-two he resumed his law practice. He was to take part in only one more murder case, one which would make him, to his distaste, a hero in the eyes of the cousins of the white supremacists against whom he had done battle in Detroit.

In 1932, Thalia Massie, the wife of a naval officer stationed at Pearl Harbor, claimed to have been raped by five Hawaiians of mixed ancestry. The racial atmosphere in Honolulu in 1932 was no better than it had been in Detroit in 1925. In 1931 over fifty cases of sexual assault against native women by American sailors had been recorded by the Honolulu police. Rarely, if ever, was any punishment given to the attacker. Accordingly, when the five alleged rapists were identified and arrested, the native authorities were not burning with zeal to prosecute them. Navy brass persisted and the five were eventually indicted for rape. The all-oriental jury could not agree, and before the defendants could be retried, Lieutenant Massie, a Virginian, his mother-in-law, Mrs. Granville Fortescue, and two sailors from Massie's command decided to administer their own brand of justice. They kidnapped, shot, and killed Joe Kahahawai, whom Thalia Massie had identified as the leader of the gang she claimed had attacked her.

Massie, Mrs. Fortescue, and the two sailors were charged with murder. Darrow, who needed money badly at that time, was not able to resist the $25,000 retainer and so in 1932 at the age of seventy-five he once again found himself at the center of a racial maelstrom. Racial fear had killed Joe Kahahawai as surely as it had killed Leon Breiner, and Darrow again set out to persuade a jury predisposed against a defendant to agree with him that bigotry and prejudice had been the killer and not the human beings in the courtroom.

Darrow's natural sympathies were with the islanders, who he said were exploited by the whites. The white man, Darrow felt, had come to Hawaii, taught the yellow and brown man to look upward to pray, and then, when the prayer was finished and the yellow and brown man looked down again, their land had been stolen from them.

The years had finally caught up with Darrow. The weariness that had always been in his face and his spirit had overtaken him and he could no longer recapture the old magic. The evidence was overwhelming that Lieutenant Massie, Mrs. Fortescue, and the two sailors had kidnapped Joe Kahahawai and that Lieutenant Massie had shot him. But, said the defense, the plan had involved only the kidnapping of Kahahawai and only to extract a confession from him. There had been no intent to commit violence. The confession, when finally extracted, had so enraged Massie that in a fit of temporary insanity he had shot and killed the victim.

As he had urged the white jury in Detroit to set aside their prejudices against the black defendants and understand their fears and hopes, so did he plead with the predominantly oriental jury in Honolulu to overcome their fears and prejudices and understand the frailty and vulnerability of the white defendants before them. The jury did not buy it. After twelve hours came the verdict—guilty of manslaughter against all defendants. Manslaughter was, indeed, a mild enough verdict since there had always been some doubt that Mrs. Massie's accusations against the five Hawaiians were entirely accurate, and even if they were, the summary disposition of Joe Kahahawai would seem to have amounted to more than manslaughter.

But not to the chauvinistic American press, which saw the trial as an evil manifestation of the yellow peril. The Hearst newspapers, which hadn't had a war of their own since 1898, were willing to start another over the Massie case. All the Hearst front pages carried this notice after the verdict:

> Write your representatives in Washington to take the necessary steps to protect the honor of American Womanhood in the American possession of Hawaii, and also to compel decent respect on the part of the Hawaiian rabble for our American nation and our nation's patriotic defenders.

One mainland correspondent reported:

> ... It is that a national danger is sensed. Political control of Uncle Sam's most important defense in the Pacific has been allowed to pass into the hands of Asiatic politicians, or politicians whose utterances and policies are based on a desire to cultivate and attract the support and advantage of the overwhelmingly Asiatic majority of the population. ...
>
> America's reply should be:
>
> Don't give up the ship!
>
> Don't give up the white women in Hawaii!
>
> Don't give up the Hawaiian Islands to Asiatic politicians!
>
> Hawaii is an American outpost!
>
> It might well be the Sumter of the next war!
>
> It should be governed by the Army or Navy of the United States in the interest and for the protection of the American nation!

The case had been an unpleasant anticlimax to Darrow's career. The racial bitterness that pervaded the trial and reverberated all the way to the mainland made it apparent that the slight ray of hope he thought he had seen after the Sweet trial was only a reflection of his own wishes. Race relations had in fact gotten worse since 1925 and Darrow was to live long enough to realize that they had not yet reached bottom.

The NAACP confidently expected, in 1926, that housing discrimination, which was rapidly making a slum out of the core of every large city in the United States, would soon be a thing of the past. *Buchanan* v. *Warley*, in 1917, had stricken down discriminatory zoning laws, at least insofar as they were explicitly based on race. The Sweet verdict, in 1926, though it did not have any special significance as a rule of law, would at least, so it was believed, serve as a warning to whites that discrimination by intimidation would no longer be an effective device for maintaining segregation. Black leaders were hopeful that the white community's third line of defense against black neighbors—restrictive covenants—would also be breached by the Supreme Court in that year. *Corrigan* v. *Buckley* had involved a typical form of agreement under which the white property owners of a neighborhood had

> ...mutually covenanted and agreed that no part of these properties should ever be used or occupied by, or sold, leased or given to, any person of the Negro race or blood; and that this covenant should run with the land and bind their respective heirs and assigns for twenty-one years from and after its date....

Agreements such as these were building an impenetrable wall around the black areas of every city in the country. The waterworks improvers were at least open and direct in their discrimination. Restrictive covenants were more subtle and sophisticated and were the product of the best ingenuity of the legal profession and the real estate industry. A white homeowner had been enjoined, in the *Corrigan* case, from violating the covenant by transferring property to a black. The Supreme Court, to the bitter disappointment of the NAACP, allowed the injunction to stand and put its stamp of respectability on the shameful business by falling back on the language of the Civil Rights cases of a half century earlier:

> It is State action of a particular character that is prohibited. Individual invasion of individual rights is not the subject matter of the amendment.

In rejecting the contention that the Thirteenth and Fourteenth Amendments prohibited such agreements the Court said:

> It is obvious that none of these amendments prohibited private individuals from entering into contracts respecting the control and disposition of their own property. . . .

The property rights that concerned the Court were, of course, the property rights of those who wished to keep their property free of the taint of black ownership. The property rights of Mrs. Corrigan, who had tried to sell her property to a black, were ignored by the Court. Mrs. Corrigan had herself signed the restrictive agreement but it would not have mattered if she hadn't since it was a "covenant running with the land."

It is difficult to tell at what point this country became irretrievably doomed to be two countries—one black and one white, separate and bitter—but several turning points stand out and at each one, until it was too late, the turn was in the wrong direction—toward repression and away from freedom.

The first was when Reconstruction died with the Tilden-Hayes electoral vote deal. Surviving Reconstruction was the Civil Rights Act by means of which Congress had attempted to put some teeth into the Thirteenth and Fourteenth Amendments. The Supreme Court neatly extracted those teeth, first numbing the patient with the anesthesia of states rights, by holding that the amendments did no more than protect the former slaves against state action. The country's white citizens could continue to be as oppressive and discriminatory against the blacks as they had always been. After all, the country seemed to be saying, we have made them free—what more do they want of us? The separate but equal doctrine of 1896 was inevitable after the Civil Rights cases, all brilliantly rationalized and justified in accordance with the best principles of strict constitutional construction.

The last clear chance to turn off this disastrous course was in the *Corrigan* case in 1926. The Marcus Garvey movement and the wave of postwar black militancy should have raised storm warnings visible to the Court, but the rough waters were confined within the inner cities and the Court chose to keep them there by fortifying the wall of separation. It was not until 1948 that the Supreme Court, in *Shelley* v. *Kraemer,* held that restrictive covenants could not be enforced since action by a court in the enforcement of such agreements constituted prohibited state action and violated the equal protection clause of the Fourteenth Amendment.

By then, of course, it was much too late. Hundreds of thousands of blacks had been crowded into the central cities with the wave of World War II black immigration from the South—central cities which were already deteriorated beyond repair. Compounding the effects of neglectful and exploitative absentee ownership was the impact of the depression when, in some cities, as much as 65 percent of the employable black males had been without work for extended periods of time. The cities had indeed become black colonies surrounded and governed, for the most part, by a ring of white suburbs or restricted white areas within the city. Blacks had little or no political leverage with which to bring about reform on their own, because malapportionment of state legislatures and city councils deprived them of the political power which their numbers should have demanded. Until the reapportionment required by the 1964 one-man one-vote decisions, small minorities—in some cases as small as 10 percent—of the population were represented in state legislative bodies by a majority of the legislators. From the time that the industrial revolution transformed this country from a rural nation to an urban nation, horses and trees were given greater representation in the state house than were people. Underrepresentation of people meant underrepresentation of cities which meant underrepresentation of blacks. It was to the tender mercy of states governed by such lily-white bodies that the Supreme Court had relegated blacks, with the States Rights philosophy that viewed the Thirteenth and Fourteenth Amendments as imposing no positive duty on the nation as a whole or on the states themselves to take affirmative action in making blacks truly equal or to prohibit acts of suppression, intimidation, or discrimination that could not be squeezed into the box labeled state action.

The *Shelley* case, though declaring state enforcement of restrictive covenants to be unconstitutional, had little effect in discouraging the continued use of such agreements. The Court, in fact, seemed to invite such use:

> Since the decision of this Court in the Civil Rights cases in 1883, 109 U.S. 3 . . . the principle has become firmly imbedded in our constitutional law that the action inhibited by the first section of the Fourteenth Amendment is only such action as may fairly be said to be that of the States. That amendment erects no shield against merely private conduct, however discriminatory or wrongful.
>
> We conclude, therefore, that the restrictive agreements standing alone cannot be regarded as violations of any rights guaranteed to petitioners by the Fourteenth Amendment. So long as the purposes of those agreements are effectuated by voluntary adherence to their terms, it would appear clear that there has been no action by the State and the provisions of the Amendment have not been violated.

Thus were born gentlemen's agreements, which, though not enforceable in a court of law, proved just as effective in keeping blacks in their place as the pre-Shelley agreements. They have proved to have remarkable durability and a high degree of social acceptance. The President of the United States in 1970 was able to shrug off a charge that his Supreme Court nominee had once been a party to such a gentlemen's agreement by casually, and without apparent regret, noting that such agreements are quite common and many fine people are parties to them.

For those with a finer sensibility and a sharper conscience than the President of the United States, more refined methods of restricting residency have been developed and widely used. These do not even require indiscreet references to race but make property transfers subject to the written consent and approval of adjoining property owners. Or elaborate building codes or architectural requirements are adopted which are rigidly applied to prospective black or other unwanted owners and at the same time readily waived for acceptable purchasers. It may or may not be true that blacks, as most whites would like to believe, really prefer to live near or with other blacks in any case, but it is certainly true that whites have expended a fantastic amount of legal, business, and social ingenuity to make damn sure that they do. Wherever blacks may prefer to live, it is clear that not much choice has been available to them in metropolitan America. The resistance to low-cost housing in suburban areas suggests that white suburbanites will not be noticeably more hospitable to black neighbors than were the good citizens of Garland and Charlevoix.

To the surprise of almost no one, the United States Commission on Civil Rights found, in the early sixties, that the practices of real estate brokers and salesmen have perpetuated patterns of housing segregation. Especially artful in this practice have been members of the Detroit Real Estate Board, the direct descendants of the waterworks improvers and the very same board which had believed so strongly that "a realtor should never be instrumental in introducing into a neighborhood . . . members of any race or nationality . . .

whose presence will be detrimental to property values. . . ."

What the Detroit board believed in 1925, it still believed in 1960 when this exchange took place between the president of the board and a member of the Civil Rights Commission:

Q: In your map you referred to the yellow area as an integrated area, and I assume that when you say the black dollar is worth more than the white dollar, you are referring to that area?

A: It buys more. It buys more housing in that whole area.

Q: In the yellow area?

A: In the yellow area.

Q: How about outside the yellow area?

A: Well, these houses on Boston Boulevard are a good example of four- and five-bedrooms, two- and three-bath houses, with a first-floor lavatory and strictly modern.

Q: That is outside the yellow area?

A: No, these are within the yellow area.

Q: I mean outside the yellow area.

A: Outside, out [in] Grand River, or in the North Woodward District out here or in Grosse Pointe, they will bring $32,000 to $35,000.

Q: Could a Negro buy it?

A: If he wants to pay the difference? I think he can. In fact, they're gradually working in that direction, but I don't know why any Negro would go out and pay $35,000 if he can buy what he can . . .

Q: No, what I am really trying to get at is whether you are, in fact, saying that the housing market in Detroit is open without regard to race or whether you are saying it is open only in a restricted area.

A: Well, it's wide open in the yellow area, and other areas are becoming open.

Q: Why should a Negro be confined to the yellow area in order to get equality?

A: . . . This is no ghetto. This is some of the finest
   housing in Detroit.

The board president then went on to explain: "As to the
role of the broker in achieving equal opportunity in housing,
we do not think this is the broker's responsibility."

When, in spite of all the ingenuity of the lawyers, the
diligence of the realtors, the covenants and agreements, a
black family manages to breach the barrier, it is still touch
and go, in most communities, whether the greeting will be by
bombs, bricks, or burning. The Sweet trial was no more successful in stopping segregation by terror than the many
NAACP cases had been in stopping segregation by legal
artifice. Darrow had done his best to warn America in 1926.
He had told the jury:

> Do not make any mistake, gentlemen. . . . I know the
> instinct for life. I know it reaches black and white
> alike. I know that you cannot confine any body of
> people to any particular place; and, as the population
> grows, the colored people will go farther, I know it,
> and you must change the law or you must take it as it
> is, or you must invoke the primal law of nature and get
> back to clubs and fists, and if you are ready for that,
> gentlemen, all right, but do it with your eyes open.

It sometimes seems the country has, indeed, gone back to
clubs and fists, and guns and mace and Molotov cocktails.
Fear and repression have fed upon each other and the suffering, sorrow, tribulation, and death among blacks and whites
prophesied by Darrow have come to pass. Fewer members
of either race seem willing to practice the patience, tolera-
tion, and understanding that he advised.

Martin Luther King, of course, was one of those who had
not yet despaired, and in his famous "I have a dream" speech
of 1963, he used Ossian Sweet's Detroit as the symbol of
housing discrimination when he said: "I have a dream this
afternoon that one day right here in Detroit Negroes will be

able to buy a house or rent a house anywhere that their money will carry them."

Ossian Sweet found that his money would not carry him to the corner of Garland and Charlevoix. He had never engaged in a sit-in or a demonstration; he had never called a cop a pig; he had never mugged or snatched a purse; he did not take dope; he was not lazy and shiftless; he never got a welfare check; he did not hate whitey; he never burned or looted; but his white neighbors were not interested in his character—only in his color. And thirty-eight years later, buying a decent house could only be a dream to Martin Luther King and is still only a dream for most blacks in every corner of this land. To white America, Eldridge Cleaver and Ossian Sweet look the same. Racial violence has enabled the country to submerge its guilt in self-righteous indignation. America has not solved its racial problems, so it has determined to ignore them. White House advisors counsel "benign neglect" and speak of the "remarkable progress" that blacks have made toward full equality.

In 1883 Justice Harlan, in his dissent in the Civil Rights cases, had warned that democratic ideals cannot survive with "any class of human beings in practical subjection to another class, with power in the latter to dole out to the former just such privileges as they may choose to grant." We have not really come very far since then. White America still, for the most part, considers justice and equality for blacks to be privileges to be doled out to blacks by whites in exchange for good behavior.

No better expression of this patronizing attitude of white America has been given than the one articulated by the President of the United States in justifying a slowdown of government initiatives in race relations in the 1970 State of the Union Address:

> It is time for those who make massive demands on
> society to make some minimal demands on themselves.

Bullshit.

Appendix

Court Cases Cited

Buchanan v. Warley, 245 U.S. 60 (1917)
Civil Rights cases, 109 U.S. 3 (1883)
Commonwealth v. Carlisle, Brightly's N.P. Rep. (Pa.) 36 (1821)
Corrigan v. Buckley, 271 U.S. 323 (1926)
Dred Scott v. Sandford, 19 How. 393 (1857)
Escobedo v. Illinois, 378 U.S. 484 (1964)
Hirabayashi v. U.S., 320 U.S. 81 (1943)
Korematsu v. U.S., 323 U.S. 214 (1944)
Miranda v. Arizona, 384 U.S. 436 (1966)
Philadelphia Cordewainers case, (1806), Reprinted in 3 Commons
   and Gilmore, Documentary History of American Industrial
   Society
Plessy v. Ferguson, 163 U.S. 537 (1896)
Rex v. Journeymen Tailors, 8 Mod. 10 (1721)
Shelley v. Kraemer, 334 U.S. 1 (1948)
State v. Birnham, 15 N.H. 396 (1844)